THE INVISIBLE
BRANSON

CREATING EXTRAORDINARY BREAKTHROUGHS

"William and Louise have this uncanny knack of turning up in my life when I need them most. When they outlined *The Invisible Branson* program to me, I thought it was just too outrageous to attempt. Looking back I can see it was foolish of me not to get on board sooner.

The most challenging part of *The Invisible Branson* process is getting out of your own way. The cynical me—that little negative voice that holds me, and many others like me, back—got in the way. My advice is to park your concerns and open your mind while you read this great book. *The Invisible Branson* will have a profound impact in your business and on your life. It changed my life, and it will change yours if you have to courage to let it.

— **Dr Brett Taylor,** *International Dental Educator and Author of "Getting Your Smile Right: The Importance of Feeling Normal"*

"I admire Richard Branson because he is a giver. As an owner of an online toyshop, I also wanted to give back. I founded a charity called *Tea4Toys* that distributes toys to underprivileged kids. But being inherently a shy person, I found it very confronting to see myself as the public face of the business and the charity.

In putting *The Invisible Branson* into practice I learned how to overcome a lot of fears, and win. Of course I am still learning and growing. If a 33-year-old mother of three can bring out her inner Branson, then anyone can!"

— **Rosalyn Manipis,** *Founder, www.ToyMadness.com.au and Tea4Toys charity*

"I decided to open my business on my 60th birthday. Now I manufacture and market the best breakfast cereal on the planet. I didn't have an ounce of marketing in me, only passion and energy for making a difference.

This is when I was introduced to *The Invisible Branson*—being a business rocker! I stepped over the chasm of unknowing, got inspired, energised, risked it all. Along the way had the time of my life. I have not looked back since.

William and Louise are the people who unlocked the inner Branson in me. I'm knocking down my barriers. It's a real buzz to stand under the spotlight now—to tell my story and share my passion on being fully alive. I really can never thank Louise and William enough."

— **Margaret Brockie,** *Maker of Brockie's Breakfast Cereals*

"I am a lawyer. As lawyers go, we tend to be about causes. Implementing *The Invisible Branson* in my life begun with my book *iWord: A Personal View On Integrity*. The game plan we mapped out is beyond anything I had thought was possible. What inspired me to put the ideas in *The Invisible Branson* into practice was, as Richard Branson said, 'Making a difference.' We all have a lot to give. The greatest thing we can give is ourselves. And this is the core message of *The Invisible Branson*. Also it's an outstanding read—easy to get through while learning a lot."

— **Gary Best,** *Partner, Clayton Utz*

"If anyone advises you that you shouldn't be the face of your business, then give them a copy of *The Invisible Branson*. Because the best thing I've done in marketing my business is to implement what is said in this book. By putting myself in the spotlight rather than having to chase business, I now have the right prospects choosing me.

And sales and marketing became fun, fun, fun. *The Invisible Branson* will unlock your full potential as a leader, marketer, and dare I say, a 'business rock star!' So read it and put it into great use."

— **Geri Forsaith** *MD, Sydney Property Conveyancing*

"You are the best person to be the face and the voice of your business. No one has the knowledge or the passion like you do. If a once-struggling baker like me from Beechworth can do this, so can you. *The Invisible Branson* gives you your roadmap on how to build a powerful brand for your business. Read this book, be inspired and never let those dream takers put a damper on your vision."

— **Tom O'Toole,** *Owner of The Beechworth Bakery, best selling author and Australia's most entertaining speaker*

"It's a no-brainer as to why you should become the face of your business. Yes, I know that so many so-called gurus will tell you that you shouldn't get so closely tied to the business. Don't let their fear and limited thinking stop you. *The Invisible Branson* will put you on a path that will rekindle your excitement for your business and life.

I am extremely impressed with *The Invisible Branson* and already implementing its principles in my life and business. Louise and William explain the why, how and what of creating a personal brand in a simple, easy way...all without the jargon so many business books are guilty of. *The Invisible Branson* is an absolute must-read for all business owners."

— **Bernie Mitchell,** *MD, Focus Property Management, Author, "Bipolar: A Path to Acceptance"*

"Today, Chiropractic Development International (CDI) is an industry leader in the continuing professional development of chiropractors. When it came to brainstorming our initial idea, branding, and promoting all aspects of CDI, we called in the services of William de Ora. He implemented *The Invisible Branson* on CDI. It is a powerful marketing blueprint.

The Invisible Branson will definitely not only challenge you to bring out your best, it will challenge your reality as you know it to be. You will be delighted you did. We sure are!"

*— **Dr Matthew Long** and **Dr Anthony Nicholson**,*
Directors of Chiropractic Development International

"I have dramatically changed how I run my accounting practice by bringing *The Invisible Branson* into my practice. I used to spend 1% of my time promoting the business now it is my number one priority.

So much so, I am authoring a book - '*How To Turn Your Business Into A Money Making Machine.*' Something I thought well beyond me. The idea of writing a book and taking centre stage at networking events was not the kind of thing you would expect from an accountant like me. By deliberately pushing myself out of my comfort zone I became very good at it! *The Invisible Branson* is more than a business book. It will shift the way you look at business and life itself!"

*— **Matthew Lee,** Director, Lee & Alexander Accountancy*

"*The Invisible Branson* is an uplifting read which challenges you to let out who you truly are. Business owners are driven by the vision of success, but hold themselves back due to fear and uncertainty. This book provides new images, concepts and permission to step outside all those negative belief patterns and soar into your true potential. It reveals the hidden power of the entrepreneur to build their personal profile into a brand and become a recognised authority in their field."

*— **Rafaele Joudry** BSW, MS (psych),* *International author and speaker,*
Founder of Sound Therapy International

"When I first read the manuscript I knew *The Invisible Branson* was an absolute must for taking any business and the entrepreneur to the stratosphere. This book unlocks Richard Branson's winning formula of how he intertwined the Virgin Brand with his own unique personality.

Louise and William brilliantly explain how to catapult yourself into becoming a business rock star in a refreshingly simple way. Every page bursts with well-thought through and immediately practical guidelines! It's magnificent!"

*— **Dr Chandler George,** Director, Dallas Internet Marketing Consulting*

THE INVISIBLE BRANSON

The Definitive Guide To Becoming a Business Rock Star

LOUISE WOODBURY
& WILLIAM DE ORA

PUBLISHED BY

QUANTUM PUBLICATIONS

The Invisible Branson represents the views of the authors. This book is not endorsed by Sir Richard Branson or the Virgin Group. Any modifications are for commercial / confidentiality reasons or simply to highlight relevant matters.

The views presented in this book are of a general nature only and do not take into account any individual circumstances.

Also by Louise Woodbury and William de Ora:
The Invisible Entrepreneur: How to Grow Your Business by Taking 3 Months Off!
ISBN 978-0-646-49043-4
The Invisible Partnership: A Blueprint For Successfully Combining Marriage & Business
ISBN 978-0-9807919-5-2

Published by Quantum Publications
First published in Australia September 2011
ISBN 978-0-980-79197-6

Quantum Publications Pty Ltd
ABN 60 076 350 635
PO Box 26, North Ryde, NSW 1670, Australia

Cover design by Phil Atkinson, Murray Vanderveer and Jon Hawley

This book is available at a discounted rate for bulk orders.
For more information, please send your enquiry to:
Ken@QuantumPublications.com.au

Websites:
www.InvisibleBranson.com
www.InvisiblePartnership.com
www.InvisibleEntrepreneur.com

First Edition
14 13 12 11   10 9 8 7 6 5 4 3 2 1

This book is dedicated to

SIR FREDDIE LAKER
(6 August 1922 – 9 February 2006)

The spirit of Sir Freddie continues…

CONTENTS

FOREWORD

BY LEE IACOCCA

I've been around long enough to know a thing or two about the importance a good role model can play in inspiring us to go above and beyond the call of duty.

In the modern business-world there are few role models that can match the intensity and brilliance of Richard Branson.

It is clear to me there are many parallels between Sir Richard Branson and myself. I see the same fighting spirit I had when I was doing the impossible at Chrysler.

Like Richard Branson I've made mistakes in my time and learned from them. That's what happens when you've been around the block a few times. In this book the lessons of Branson's life are distilled with conciseness and clarity and I suspect it will act as a wake-up call for many!

We all know these are hard times and it is impossible to miss the sense of anxiety that haunts the business community. I agreed to write the foreword for *The Invisible Branson* because there are lessons in this book that are essential.

In this book we get a glimpse of a world where you can make a difference without exploiting people and a world where it is possible to turn a handsome profit and remain a decent person.

Like Sir Richard I have always believed that in life there are times when you have to take the risk and take on fights that seem to be unwinnable. I decided early on that I would never shy away from these battles. It's not just good business but when principles are at risk, the right thing to do.

I see the same fighting spirit in Richard Branson and you too can learn to unlock it.

This book is designed to show you how to do just that. It'll take some gutsy decisions on your part, but I guarantee you that it will open your eyes to a new way of doing business.

Louise and William demonstrate this point by showing that all the great business leaders of our time share this one quality of gutsiness.

In these pages you will find countless examples of people making a difference by acting in concert with their own fundamental principles. It all comes down to how you look at the world and tap into that part of yourself that has been asleep.

If you want to wake up from your slumber make sure to crack open these pages and embark on a journey with one of the greatest business leaders of modern time.

It is time to make the leap you have promised yourself you will one day make. *The Invisible Branson* will show you how to make this happen.

Lee Iacocca
Author of "Where Have All the Leaders Gone?"

The Iacocca Family Foundation funds innovative and promising diabetes research programs and projects that will lead to a cure for the disease and alleviate complications caused by it.

CHAPTER ONE

You Don't Need a Guitar to Be a Rock Star

Are you ready to take on a whole new level of personal and business success? Are you ready to learn how to attract new customers to your business rather than hunt for them? Are you ready to become a "rock star" in your professional niche?

Let's get straight to the point. You're reading this book because you want to know how to make your company grow and thrive. That's what we want for you as well.

Today, business owners have a remarkable opportunity in the new economy to take advantage of a powerful marketing tool called personal branding. To develop a personal brand is, in summary, a process of making yourself the public face of your business.

Before the thought of exposing yourself—a mere mortal—as an advertising mechanism frightens you, let us explain what personal branding is and what it isn't, and why personal branding can be such a powerful strategy for small business entrepreneurs in today's global economy.

First of all, personal branding is not about creating an exaggerated or false representation of yourself. Nor is it about developing a facade just to attract clients. To the contrary, great personal brands are built on the foundation of your expertise and true self—your strengths, experience, capacity, character, and values.

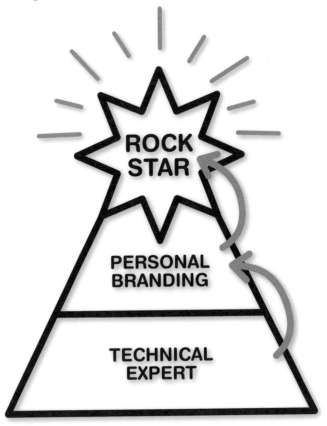

Technical Expert: valuing what you know, and what you're good at.
Personal Branding: making yourself the public face of your business.
Rock Star: becoming the authority in your niche.

Personal branding is first and foremost a marketing tool. It is the public presentation of the *real you*. This *real you* is a very powerful marketing tool for producing increased sales in your business!

That said, the purpose of developing a personal brand is about growing your business into a thriving and profitable venture. And, it can help your business grow in ways you never thought possible.

Personal Branding: A Powerful Marketing Tool No One Else Can Own

The basics in business will always remain the same. For you to succeed, you must grab the attention of prospective clients. You have to let the world know that you exist and that you have the products and services they're looking for. Any sales guru will tell you that this is the first step. Without attracting more customers you cannot increase your sales. It's always been the case!

But a lot has changed in business and marketing. Among other factors, the Internet and globalization have opened new doors of opportunity for businesses to sell products and services globally. At the same time, globalization has also increased competition. So, the challenge for small business owners today is to figure out how to take advantage of the broader market while facing the challenge of increased competition.

The solution is to develop a strong personal brand and begin to communicate with your target market about who you are and why you do what you do—what you care most about. Everyone competing to get a tiny piece of your customer's mind. Your customer is bombarded with information, propaganda, e-mail spam, TV commercials, website banners, Google ads, and junk mail.

The problem really is this: All those traditional marketing approaches are impersonal. The customer has no connection to the company and they aren't sure which business to *trust*.

Trust: The Most Important Advantage That Small Business Owners Have

At a core level, buying and selling is a *relational* transaction. Like any relationship, it requires trust. Traditional marketing can help get the word out about your products and services. However, the Achilles heel is that it's ineffective in building trust between you and your clients.

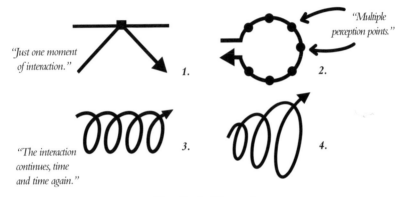

"Just one moment of interaction." 1.

"Multiple perception points." 2.

"The interaction continues, time and time again." 3.

4.

Up Your Service! Interactions

1. One-shot deal - *There is only one relatively short moment of interaction.* **2. Transaction satisfaction** - *Many perception points or 'moments of truth' occur where quality of service is assessed.* **3. Reliable relationships** - *Both parties prove themselves to be dependable, reliable and consistent. These are the people and companies you can count on, time and time again.* **4. Powerful relationships** - *Both parties obtain greater value over time. The partnership becomes more important, positive, productive, prosperous, profitable and proactive. Copyright, Ron Kaufman – C1:1*

So, how do you grab the attention of potential customers *and* build trust in a genuine and sincere way?

First and foremost we recommend that you separate yourself from your competitors by becoming the personal brand of your company. This is no different than what Sir Richard Branson has successfully achieved with the Virgin brand.

We all know that customers do business with people they trust. And, trust is built when the customer feels like they know what you stand for, why you do what you do, and have a sense that you are someone with integrity.

Customers equally trust people who are experts in their field. They trust real people with real faces. Therefore, becoming a recognized authority in your business niche is a key to gaining the trust of your clients.

Would You Trust a Rock Star

Let's turn to the world of rock. Would you trust a rock star? Well, it probably depends on which one. However, whether you trust a rock star or not, most have figured out how to grab and keep the attention of their audience—their customers.

Rock stars use many personal branding techniques to attract music lovers around the world. However, their main focus is on getting attention rather than winning trust. As Gene Simmons of the rock band KISS said, "James Bond has a license to kill; rock stars have a license to be outrageous. Rock is about grabbing people's attention." [C1:2]

What we propose in this book is that you—the business entrepreneur—apply a rock star personal branding strategy to get the attention of *your* potential customers. But we don't want you to stop there. We want you to use the personal branding strategies of Sir Richard Branson, the rock star entrepreneur, so that you not only attract attention to your company but also win the trust of your clients.

From the outset, let's be clear that becoming a "rock star" in your business niche has nothing to do with going on an ego trip. Inflated egos don't attract anybody.

What we propose in this book is not about becoming someone you're not. Becoming a rock star is simply about promoting yourself as *the* authority and expert in your field. The purpose of your personal brand is to educate your customers about *why* they should be doing business with you—it's simply about you sharing your story with them.

Taking a Stand

It's about you being willing to take a stand based on what's important to you. It's about ensuring that your reason for becoming an entrepreneur is fully realized. It's about putting the spotlight on your unique skills, talents and value, to ensure that you attract the right clients for the right reasons.

And this is exactly why we have chosen to base this book on one of the most successful, most visible business achievers of our time—Sir Richard Branson.

From our observations, we believe that one of the key reasons why Sir Richard Branson has been so successful in business is because he wants to do the right thing by ordinary, every day folks. And this is what inspires us about him and his organization.

In a nutshell, when you think of Sir Richard you think of Virgin—they are one and the same. And this is the power of personal branding.

From our perspective, we also believe that it is possible for every entrepreneur to tap into the success strategies of people such as Branson and follow in their footsteps.

We trust that you're starting to see the connection between rock stars, Branson, and you. But let's go a little deeper into this topic.

Your Name: The Most Important Element of Your Brand

The importance of personal branding in today's global economy was revealed by the international best selling authors Al Ries and Jack Trout in their book *Positioning: The Battle For Your Mind*. "Your name is your primary weapon in the battle for the mind," they wrote. [C1:3]

Did you catch that? Your *name* is the key to successful marketing This means that in order to own a piece of your customer's mind, you need a personal brand, at least if you are going to position yourself above your competition as the most desirable option in the marketplace.

This is exactly what Walter Landor, a pioneer in branding and consumer research was also referring to when he said, "Products are created in the factory, but brands are created in the mind." [C1:4]

The harsh reality is this: Our customers don't wake up thinking about us; they are busy thinking about what is important to them. And they have their own problems, challenges and concerns—just as you have yours.

To be a successful small business owner, you need to establish yourself in your customer's mind. Which means you must first get their attention—by having *real* conversations with them—in order to gain their trust.

At the end of the day, your customers and prospects buy from you, not because your products or services are necessarily superior (although we hope they are), but because they feel like they know you. If people believe in what you believe in, they'll do business with you. Human beings make decisions based on how they feel. They also do business with people they can have a great relationship with.

This book is designed to help you build your business, through personal branding. And, Sir Richard Branson is one of the best-known examples of a business leader who uses personal branding to grow his businesses. But he is by no means the only business owner to use the technique of branding himself to succeed in his business ventures.

Consider Paul Newman, in the context of his natural foods company. Or real estate mogul Donald Trump. And, of course, the technique has long been known to actors, sports stars, and celebrities, such as American television host, actress, producer, philanthropist Oprah Winfrey, golfer Greg Norman, tennis legend Andre Agassi, supermodel Elle Macpherson, musician Kylie Minogue, and soccer champion David Beckham.

Your Face Generates Trust

Another legendary self-branding success story was Victor Kiam, former owner of the Remington Razor company. Instead of featuring the razor in his ads, he featured himself. When he famously stated, "I liked it so much, I bought the company," he made himself the face of Remington Razor and built trust with the public. [C1:5]

The common thread among these personal branding champions is that they all began as "attention-grabbing rock stars." However, they have evolved into *trustworthy*, attention-grabbing rock stars.

In business, the only thing that lasts is brand recognition—because brand recognition generates trust. You can implement the "rock star" technique by developing brand recognition around your own name, face, personality, expertise, and relevant opinions.

By comparison, time and money spent on advertising your products or services is essentially wasted. Sure, it might bring you some clients in the short-term, but the surge won't last. Old style advertising will never match the credibility factor you can gain by emulating an entrepreneur like Branson.

After many years of providing coaching and mentoring services for small businesses, we have seen first-hand great companies depend on great leaders and great teams. In the new global economy, there is a remarkable opportunity today for small businesses to grow, to become more profitable, and to have an impact on the community.

But this opportunity often requires the business owner to undergo profound personal change. In today's world, a thriving small business depends on a thriving business owner.

Personalizing Your Business is the Key

Real personal branding, as we said, requires authenticity. It's not about creating a facade. This is one of the key factors in Sir Richard Branson's success story. What you see in the public arena from Branson is what you get from the Virgin Group. There is alignment and congruency between the personal values of Branson and the core values of the business.

For this reason, developing a sincere, authentic personal brand is for many small business owners a revolutionary shift in thinking. However, it's perhaps the most invigorating and exciting process that a business owner can pursue.

Why? Because you will be able to ensure that your business is an authentic expression of your deepest beliefs and values. As you rise to new heights as a person, you will simultaneously lift your business to new heights.

Greatness—both personal and business—is ultimately what *The Invisible Branson* is about. True greatness is never inauthentic. Best-selling author Jim Collins makes it clear in his speeches and books that greatness does not depend on circumstances—the cards you have been dealt. To the contrary, greatness is possible when leaders develop a spirit and culture of discipline, first in themselves and then in their companies. [C1:6]

Any business owner—no matter how well your company is doing now—can grow and thrive. Running a great company *is* an accessible goal.

Personal branding is definitely one of the ways Sir Richard Branson has developed his business empire. What few people realize, however, is that his approach to life and business is also possible for small business owners. No entrepreneur ought to consider the concept of becoming an authority in their field—and to make money while having fun—as something beyond them.

It is not an unreachable or out-there goal. However, you do

need to translate your self-belief into action.

Perhaps you're someone who already senses the need for change and personal growth. Or you may be a business owner whose company is coasting along at a comfortable level, and you've been content with that for many years.

Either way, we believe that by reading this book you'll be awakened to new and previously unimagined possibilities. We hope this book will spur you to re-examine your life and company, and to consider the pursuit of greatness.

Toward a Future with New Possibilities

For some people, the very thought of creating a personal brand can be daunting. It is much easier to create a brand for your business because the business is a "thing." However, when it comes to doing the same for yourself, you're suddenly way out of your comfort zone. If you think that frightening feeling can only happen to you, then do yourself a favor and read *Losing My Virginity*, Sir Richard Branson's autobiography. [C1:7]

Even someone like Branson has his moments of doubt; but he has had the fortitude and persistence to overcome them. Like him, you need to have faith—faith in yourself and belief in the goals you are setting out to achieve.

In the next chapter we will share two case studies that demonstrate what drives and shapes the personal branding process.

One of these case studies is about William's personal situation and how a major decision forced him to re-examine his life. This led him to abandon erroneous notions of himself and then live according to his true self—including in his business.

Prior to all the changes in my life, I (William) experienced a time of resounding frustration. I had unexpectedly come to learn that there was more inside me than I was unleashing into the world. For this reason, it does not surprise me that most entrepreneurs come up with their best work when they are faced with a fork in the road—one that always forces them to grapple with their true identity. And, I am no different.

In the next chapter, allow me to tell you why.

CHAPTER TWO

CREATING YOUR PERSONAL BRAND

As we said in Chapter One, the key focus in this book is about learning to take full advantage of a powerful marketing tool called personal branding and using it to catapult you into becoming a business rock star through making yourself the public face of your business.

This is not about creating an artificial persona. On the contrary, the process of developing a personal brand is actually about discovering your true essence and identity—your strengths, talents, character, personality and values—and then expressing that identity into your market.

As we said, to show you how this works, we'd like to share two case studies about what drives and shapes the personal branding process. The first case study is based on our client John Shanahan. The second is about William's personal journey.

Story of John Shanahan

John is the CEO and owner of a company called Pyrosales. The company makes industrial temperature sensors. In recent years, John's business received the Suncorp Western Sydney Business of the Year Award. Not only did he receive this prestigious award, the business was also recognized with the Award for Excellence in Exporting and simultaneously was a finalist in the Premier's New South Wales Export awards.

These are all great achievements. However, the reason for sharing this with you is that these acknowledgments are far more significant when you come to understand the obstacles that John overcame to earn them.

In March 2006, just three years before he won the awards, Pyrosales was in administration! Then the global financial crisis put the company's Australian market share under even greater threat. Clients were deferring orders. Like similar manufacturers, Shanahan faced the daunting prospect of retrenching staff and cutting back.

However, rather than focusing on the obstacles, he took on our guidance of channeling his "inner Branson" and chose to look for new possibilities. He started to ask "What if?" questions such as: If the Australian market was in decline, then what could he do to get a share of the world market?

The answer: He needed to go from thinking of himself and his business as small timers and begin the journey of operating like the world's best in his niche. He needed to create a personal brand that would become known in the global market in which Pyrosales would operate. And, he had no time to waste!

It was do or die time: to admit defeat and face the crisis of administration, or use the fact of being cornered and come out fighting. John chose to fight. He decided to create a clear and

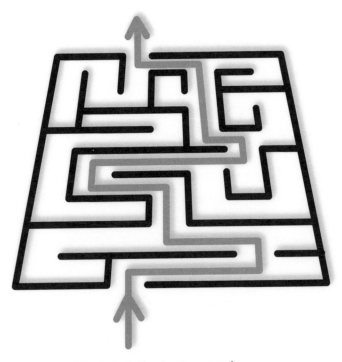

When faced with life's adversities, most people
choose to work their way through the maze.

compelling goal that not only inspired him as the CEO, but also would have the same effect on his team, clients, and prospects alike.

At first, the notion of gaining a world market share seemed unrealistic. After all, he'd need to become the best in the world to get any recognition. The biggest obstacle was navigating through his mindset (beliefs and perceptions) of how his small organization, in the back streets of suburban Sydney, could take on the world market. Thankfully, John was up for the challenge.

He knew that to be the best, his first priority was to understand the needs of the global market. This could not be done from his desk. So, with a sense of urgency, he visited fifteen countries and about thirty-six business prospects in a matter of months.

The purpose of these visits was not to sell anything. It was

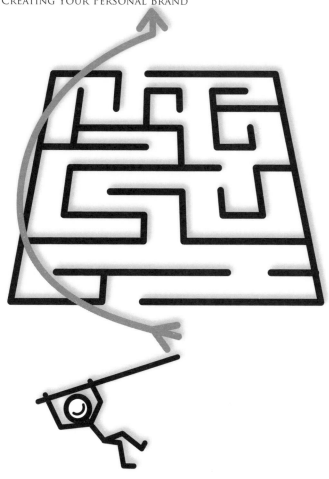

Or, the Branson way would be to be bold and
audacious and pole volt yourself to the other side.

about understanding their needs and requirements so he could begin to build relationships based on trust. And, in time, give him the opportunity to sell from a position of strength.

As is the case with most business-to-business connections, when a client senses your true commitment to gaining an understanding of what's important to them, they invite you in. The act of clocking up thousands upon thousands of flying hours certainly grabbed the attention of his prospects. It opened doors that were otherwise difficult to get through.

John literally touched, moved, and inspired his counterparts through his commitment and willingness to take the initiative to get into their world. And in the process of visiting all these businesses, he became known as the world's most knowledgeable person in his field.

The results were spectacular. During the height of the financial crisis, John's business gained a million dollars in extra revenue. And we're sure you'd like to know what made this sort of turnaround possible?

The first key is that when we work with our clients, we encourage them to embrace one of Richard Branson's principles: "Be bold but don't gamble." C2:1

The second key is that as coaches and mentors we don't preach theory. We only ever advise our clients to do what we have either done or would be prepared to do in our own business.

And we know that to take bold steps you need to be congruent with yourself. That is, to know who you truly are— and to be at ease in your own skin.

Story of William de Ora

To illustrate the importance of being truly congruent with yourself, we now want to share with you William's personal story:

I was born in Colombo, Sri Lanka, and given the birth name of William de Silva. As my parents had divorced when I was three, I lived with my father until his death. I was raised as a doctor's son and underwent a somewhat peculiar education that confusingly combined Christianity with Buddhism.

However, at the age of twelve (when my father died) I was sent to the United Kingdom to live with my mother. To paint you an even clearer picture, I could not speak English, and I was neither black nor white, but rather a brown-skinned boy who was excited by a new adventure. I was, upon reflection, naive about the real world.

My most valuable life lessons occurred when I had the rather dubious honor of being beaten up by both white English kids and black West Indian kids. I felt I didn't fit in with any group.

In my early twenties I snapped up an opportunity to emigrate from the United Kingdom to Australia and was fortunate to land a great job in the advertising industry. In hindsight that job was a godsend. I went on to spend twenty-five years of my life as an art director working for some of the largest and most creative advertising agencies in the country.

My position involved coming up with new ideas about how to advertise and promote our clients' products. Every day was all about creating new identities for all types of products. I was given a blank sheet of paper and expected to come up with a new look and meaning for the brand, and I was handsomely paid to do so.

This may sound like an ideal job, and in many ways it was. But by 1989 the world of advertising was changing, and more importantly, I was changing. In 1990 I decided to leave my career and start my own business.

The Catalyst for Change

I was in my early forties and while I had lived the high life, travelled the world for twenty-five years, and had a lot of fun, I didn't have too much to show for it. I worked hard but played equally hard. There was definitely no tomorrow—or so I thought!

I remember waking up one day and realizing that while I had been busy making other people successful, I was now facing the reality that I hadn't taken care of my own future.

I was flat broke and depressed. I really didn't know how I was going to make my rent payments, and my future seemed dull. While I could easily have maintained a facade of success, I knew I needed to do something different.

I confronted the fact that I had sold myself short to be able to succeed in the business world and that I had squandered many opportunities. I felt I had wasted so much of my life.

Miserable, with increasingly dark visions, I contemplated taking the easy way out. Thankfully a voice inside me kept whispering that there was hope—but only if I decided to leave my old life behind and create a new one.

It was time for action. My background, life experiences, skills and knowledge all came to the forefront. I realized that if I was this unhappy with my life, then I had to choose: either find another job or be prepared to back myself and create a whole new reality. There was no point in continuing to waste my time, spin my wheels, or keep berating myself.

When faced with this predicament, most people consider new jobs, or decide to move to a new city or a different country. However, I knew I needed a total, personal 360-degree overhaul. And, as most of our clients know, I don't do things in small measures.

Going for Gold

I began to do for myself what I had so often done for my clients: I would *rebrand* myself. I would create a totally new persona and then challenge myself to step into that identity. I knew that if I could rebrand myself, then the sky was the limit. There was nothing to be gained in settling for average or ordinary!

This meant considering the possibility of something as fundamental as a name change. As I mentioned before, my birth name was de Silva. And I was absolutely certain that I wanted more than just silver in my future. My life would be about going for gold.

And so the name "de Ora" was born. (This name is created from *Di Oro* or *d'oro,* which is the Italian translation for "of gold." In French, the word *Or* means gold, and *d'or* means of gold.) I changed my name by deed poll on 30 April 1992 and reinvented myself as William de Ora. I gave myself permission to become the person I had always wanted to be.

But let me be straight with you. From my perspective, I had my back to the wall at the time. What I know now is that you need not wait to hit rock bottom in order make changes. It is far more enjoyable to intentionally create a personal brand when life is great.

For me, it was important to understand what success meant in my life. To make changes to my identity was not about some ego trip. It was about reclaiming my true self.

The process of rebranding and reinvention was about peeling off the old facades I had built up in order to fit in. It was a process of discovering and giving value to my true self. It was about being responsible for my life. After all, I was the writer, director, and star of my life.

The difference between William de Silva and William de Ora is that the latter is far more congruent with the spirit of who I am. In coming to Australia, I wanted desperately to be accepted. So I did everything I knew to become an Australian. Inevitably, somewhere along the way, I lost my identity—and any real sense of who I actually was.

Unfortunately, and all too often, we see this happening with many small business entrepreneurs. They start out with inspiration, motivation, passion, and purpose only to become numb, frustrated, and very disillusioned by their businesses. However, it really doesn't need to be this way.

This is why Sir Richard Branson is a fantastic role model because, as he describes in his book, *Screw It, Let's Do It; Lessons In Life* "If something stops being fun, I ask *why?* If I can't fix it, I stop doing it." [C2:2]

Reincarnation—In This Lifetime

Changing my surname allowed me to express all the positive attributes I had ever wanted. It was a stunning revelation that I could actually step into that new identity. But, as I now realize, it wasn't just about changing my name. It was about breaking away from the past. I had the freedom to focus on the future and start working with a clean slate.

For me, this was like going on a holiday. I'm sure you've experienced a different way of being while on vacation. You feel a freedom and ease with life—different from how you normally are. Everything around you looks fresh, clean and interesting. You have a sense of joy and curiosity about life. You do and say things you would normally never think of doing and saying. Even if you make a fool of yourself, it doesn't matter because no one knows you.

When I invented William de Ora, this is exactly how I felt. It transformed me; but unlike a vacation, this new life direction wouldn't end. It was the new, real me, and I could now look forward to an endless future, free from all the baggage of the past.

Meaning of Life

What I created is not that unusual. However, what became clear to me is that the meaning of *my* life is all about the meaning I give it. And as I became more secure in my true self, I was able to extend my identity into my business and work. My personal brand emerged and grew, and I became a recognized expert.

Perhaps you're thinking that you're not really an expert. You see yourself as a businessperson, just like any other. If this is correct, then we are here to tell you that if you have been running your business for more than five years, you know a lot. It's time to move into the spotlight and share your knowledge.

In the coming chapters, we'll show you exactly how to do that.

In your case, you may not want to change your name, however what we want you to consider is what it would take for you to go from "Mr/Mrs. Average Business Owner" to "The Rock Star" in your niche?

Becoming Self-Congruent

The new life I (William) created was that of a business mentor/ coach. I decided to use a methodology that suited me to a tee. Something that combined the philosophies I knew best. The perfect marriage—east and west. This evolved into a fusion of a deeply grounding Buddhist philosophy coupled with my passion and excellence in marketing and advertising.

By combining the two, I cleared a new and productive path. It was a path that would add *value* to what I could offer my clients. I came to realize that the color of my skin was perfect for this role. It gave me a point of difference.

I knew how to package this new identity and simply gave myself the same advice I had given to my clients. I was learning how to operate from a mindset of success versus one of survival mode. This brought new difficulties and challenges.

It also required considerable adjustment. But as a result of redefining my life, I had the fortunate opportunity of meeting my wife and business partner, Louise. In so many ways, life turned around for me when I *decided* to turn it around.

Of course I still had self-doubts, but the feedback I received from my clients was stunning. At times I couldn't believe what I was hearing from them. Looking back I understand that the reason for my success is that I finally became congruent with who I am at heart, the person I had always wanted to be. My true identity then became congruent with every other aspect of my life—in business and in relationships.

Sir Richard Branson exemplifies this self-congruency, as do other well-known business leaders such as Donald Trump, Oprah Winfrey, Martha Stewart, and Warren Buffett. It's all about being true to yourself in all your endeavors and dealings. It has nothing to do with money. It's about being aligned with your heart, your spirit, and your soul.

Why I Chose to Change

The reason for sharing my personal story with you is because I want you to understand that developing your personal brand and becoming an authority in your profession does not mean inventing some facade that's not based on who *you* really are.

This is something that Louise and I have discussed and debated many times. It's crucial that you understand that developing a personal brand should be based on your true self. Having discovered that essence, you will be able to live life fully, and authentically in your business.

It is fair to suppose that you know more about yourself and your business than you realize. We believe you're already an authority in your market. But we speculate that you may not necessarily grasp your own credibility or, for that matter your true value.

Louise and I have encountered many people who have amazing capabilities and experience but they fail to recognize their own resources or worth. Or, if they are aware of their capacity, they often deny its true value.

Young people are usually less timid about recognizing their value and abilities than older professionals. William used to lead motivational classes for teenagers. One of the exercises he gave these students was to have them write down two hundred good things about themselves.

This simple exercise would take approximately half an hour

at best. Interestingly, when the same exercise is undertaken by business owners, it usually takes anywhere between a week or two, and even then they struggle.

The point here is that as we grow older, we all tend to accumulate a great deal of baggage. Most likely you have no problem identifying what is not okay about you but you struggle to see what is good.

This is what had happened to me (William). I knew all the reasons why my life *wasn't* working. I had organized my life so that there was supporting evidence for the thesis that I wasn't a success. I was trapped. And, for me, the way out was to change my identity.

It is worth noting though, that there is a vast difference between what I have done and what someone like Madonna has done in order to keep her audience engaged and keep the spotlight shining brightly on her. Madonna is forever changing her image, whether she is a good girl gone bad, a virgin in white, a Marilyn Monroe, a 1920s gangster moll, an androgynous person, a cold robot, a naked sex symbol, a glamor queen, a cosmic spirit, or, finally, a doting mother.

Her ability to change images every couple of years has fascinated the world, and it has been vital to her financial success. But it's not what I did, nor is it what this book is about.

Underneath the Facade

Our approach to personal branding starts with peeling away the layers of your facade in order to gain access to the real you. Only *you* will know who that real you is. I gained closer access to my real self by developing my personal brand, according to my true identity.

In John Shanahan's case, he didn't have the luxury of time to peel away his mild demeanor. Just like John, you too have what it takes to break through those invisible barriers between you and the success you dream of.

We recognize that there can be a sense of vulnerability in exposing one's true self in the rough and tumble world of business. For this reason, we take enormous strength in seeing how Sir Richard Branson turned the world upside down without having to conform or pretend to be anyone but himself. It's for this reason that we chose to focus on his life as a role model for the principles in this book.

In the next section of this book, we will spend several chapters helping you to discover the real you. Don't be concerned: our discussion is open-ended and designed to give you a framework for self-discovery and developing a personal brand.

The main thing to remember is that your true identity is the foundation for helping you develop your personal brand and be the recognized expert in your field.

And that will help you become the most authentic business "rock star" around.

CHAPTER THREE

THE POWER OF
YOUR MIND

"I can't do this. It's impossible. It's just too big," Luke told Yoda in one of the early Star Wars movies. Lacking a sense of humor, Yoda looked disappointed. "It's not the size of that thing that's important. You must unlearn what you've learned," Yoda explained.

But Luke continued saying it was impossible. Yoda paused, centered himself, and then used his mind to lift the X-wing craft from the mud and set it safely on the ground. Luke was stunned.

"I don't believe it!" he said.

"And that," said Yoda, "is why you fail." C3:1

That famous exchange between Yoda and Luke Skywalker demonstrates the power of our minds. Every day we have a choice. You can think that anything is possible, or you can think that everything is impossible.

When you first started out in business, you would have had an "anything is possible" mindset. This provided you with the impetus to create the business you currently have. What you have built to date gives you an insight into how you've used the power of your mind. So take a look around and acknowledge your successes. Be very grateful for what you do have. Know that this is your foundation—the platform from which to create your next stage.

To become a publicly recognized authority in your field, the rock star in your market, you must believe in your ability, your worth, and your goals. You cannot devalue or undermine your talents.

Let's look at the type of mindset and the attitude you'll need when developing your personal brand.

BHAG: Big Hairy Audacious Goal

To become the rock star in your field you must understand the importance of creating goals that inspire you into action. These goals need to be big, hairy, and audacious.

If you've never heard of this expression before today, then we highly recommend you read *Built to Last*, the best seller by James Collins and Jerry Porras.

Collins and Porras coined the term "big, hairy, audacious goal (BHAG)," which they described as follows: "A BHAG engages people—it reaches out and grabs them in the gut. It is tangible, energizing, highly focused. People 'get it' right away; it takes little or no explanation." [C3: 2]

In short, a BHAG is different from your traditional organizational goals and objectives. A BHAG is way bigger—it's the huge overarching goal for which every other goal serves.

Collins and Porras suggest you will know a BHAG by

identifying the following characteristics:

- *It should be so clear and compelling that it requires little or no explanation.*
- *It should fall well outside the comfort zone. People in the organization should have reason to believe they can pull it off, yet it should require heroic effort and perhaps even a little luck.*
- *It should be so bold and exciting in its own right that it would continue to stimulate progress even if the organization's leaders disappeared before it had been completed.*
- *It should be consistent with the company's core ideology.*
- *BHAGs have a long time frame—ten to thirty years.*

A BHAG is like your bucket list. This is a list of out-of-reach goals that, if achieved, would blow your mind. However, they would allow you to look back and acknowledge that you really went for it and lived life to the max. No stone was ever left unturned.

For entrepreneurs there is never a shortage of big ideas and dreams. And for the average human being they may often seem a bit crazy. This is why it is so important for you to have in your mind's eye a picture of what your life is really about and why you choose to do what you do.

In deciding to become a rock star, you are the one who needs to be inspired by this. If you are not inspired by your own goals, there is no way that you will inspire others. You are the source and the spirit of your goal—its veritable essence.

You need to be committed to doing whatever it takes to make it a reality. Along the way there will be a million and one people who won't believe that it's possible for you to achieve this. This is why we see so many entrepreneurs become numb, frustrated, and disillusioned with their dreams. They want people to believe in them. They want support from the people who are close to them. However, what you must realize is that if you dare to dream big, you inadvertently dare the people closest to you to dream big. And not everyone is up for living an extraordinary life.

Whether you currently realize it or not, you have the qualities required to become an inspiring leader. The key to your success is whether you are ready to create a new possibility for your business and yourself. Are you ready to be an inspiration? Are you ready to create *your* big hairy audacious goal?

Your Willingness to Take Risks

Actor Will Smith, in an interview with Oprah Winfrey, said, "Greatness lives on the edge of destruction, and the reason someone is great is that they have survived death."[C3:3] Will Smith could easily have been describing Sir Richard Branson.

If you think about it, what this statement really means is, that the challenges we face will test us. They show us what we're made of. Most challenges provide us with the opportunity to see that we are far greater than we ever think we are. What you need to evaluate is: do you have what it takes to pursue your goals, regardless of your circumstances? Are you willing to give up your excuses and stop yelling, "The sky is falling?"

Entrepreneurs consistently encounter tough situations. Staring into the face of failure, our backs against the wall, we might whimper for a moment but manage to dig deep into an inner reserve to gain the strength needed to conquer the fear and get back on top.

Learning to be a business rock star is a matter of extending that principle. You need the intention and the will to push yourself to take the leap to greatness. You cannot be in the mindset of waiting for something to go wrong. Instead of aiming to just survive a looming threat, you need to aim for outrageous success.

French poet and playwright Guillaume Apollinaire had this to say about making such a leap:

> *"Come to the edge.*
> *We can't. We're afraid.*
> *Come to the edge.*
> *We can't. We will fall!*
> *Come to the edge.*
> *And they came.*
> *And he pushed them.*
> *And they flew."* [C3:4]

To become a business rock star, you need to take a leap. This will require a willingness to leave your comfort zone: that warm, cozy, and nurturing place you might have been occupying for some time.

Responsibility and Accountability

In the previous chapter, I (William) described my personal process of discovering my true identity. But even with my newfound identity not everything went as planned. Life remained a roller coaster ride. However, this time, I simply decided that I'd refuse to blame someone else for my situation because I knew it was entirely my responsibility. I needed to hold myself to account to achieve all the things that I wanted.

It was tempting to revert back to my old habits. But I had made a commitment to myself not to default to my previous way of operating.

If your business isn't where you think it should be, then there is no one else to blame. It's totally your responsibility. Assuming responsibility is a topic we have covered in our previous books, *The Invisible Entrepreneur* and *The Invisible Partnership*. Since this is a core principle we teach, here is an overview of what assuming responsibility is about.

Now, let's be straight; no one else can live your life for you. So one of the first things we all need to do to embark on the track of success is to overcome the sense of denial that makes us blame others for our problems.

The Solution Needs to Come from Within

Even when problems are external, the solution to a problem still needs to come from within us. If you are not happy with the way things are, if your life isn't everything you want it to be, then it is up to you to transform it.

I am adamant about this truth because it became blindingly clear to me in my darkest hour, when my thoughts turned to suicide. This is when I got my act together and realized that if anyone was going to sort out my life then it would have to be me.

What I know for sure is that once you decide to accept responsibility for yourself, you feel as though a burden has been lifted from your shoulders. Your self-esteem increases and you develop a new fighting spirit. You come to realize that you deserve a place in this world. The act of accepting responsibility is an act of maturity, empowerment, and growth.

In my case, I stopped sabotaging myself and put my subconscious demons back into their box. I also became less of a silverback male gorilla with other people and began earning, or regaining, their respect and willingness to cooperate.

This all sounds very easy, but I understand how difficult it can be to uproot the weeds of insecurity, fear, arrogance, old habits, ingrained prejudices, lack of self-esteem and, potentially, many others. Albert Schweitzer had this to say about taking responsibility: "Man must cease attributing his problems to his environment, and learn again to exercise his will—his personal responsibility." C3:5

Another wise soul, the ancient Greek playwright Sophocles, said: "It is a painful thing to look at your own trouble and know that you yourself and no one else has made it." C3:6

Set Your Own Standards of Success

Reaching beyond your current limits and setting standards for your own greatness depends entirely on you. You can set the bar as high as you want. It is truly up to you. All we invite you to think about is to go beyond your comfort zone. As business coaches and mentors, we always ask of our clients just a bit more than they ask of themselves. As they progress, we ask them to reach for more again, and again, until they fly.

However, you must have a clear definition of what success means to you. While you can gain insights from others, you cannot fall into the trap of comparing yourself to others. Your life's journey can only ever be about discovering your personal standard of success.

Life can be described as a series of challenges that make us learn and grow. With each challenge you learn more about yourself. In effect, life is about creation and adventure rather than about cowering within your comfort zone.

We often learn the most about ourselves when we're pushed

to the limits of our personal capacity. The phrase "Greatness lives on the edge of destruction" means that pushing beyond your comfort zone will help destroy old boundaries. And in doing so, you discover a new you—greater aspects of yourself that you didn't know existed.

Business rock stars such as Sir Richard Branson have taken this to the extreme. They get a thrill from stretching themselves past what they think is possible, then achieving their goal, then stretching themselves yet again. They never stop until they reach the pinnacle.

Branson's level of success may or may not be for you. The point is to not compare your desired level of business success with someone who is shooting for the moon if you're only aiming for the mountaintop. The results of your efforts won't be the same, but there is nothing wrong with that, so long as the mountaintop is truly as far as you choose to go. Whatever level you aim for, you still must break through your comfort zone, all the way up the hill, until you reach the target you've set for yourself.

The Difference Between Richard Branson and You

The difference between you and Branson might be similar to the difference between someone who takes part in a fun run versus an Olympic athlete. It's not that one is more important than the other. It's just that they both seek different outcomes and therefore different levels of achievement. In other words, the measure of your success depends on your own yardstick, not on the standards of others.

In our minds, we believe you are already great and on a path of self-discovery. What we want to challenge you on is, are you reaching your full potential? Where you stand in relation to others is not important.

Remember the famous quote by the great Italian artist Michelangelo, when asked about the process of sculpturing

David: "Every block of stone has a statue inside it, and it is the task of the sculptor to discover it." [C3:7]

The innermost you is also a work of art. You have only to see it, and then chip away at the things that keep it from being visible to the world. Like the statue hidden within the stone, your greatness exists whether or not you realize it and unlock it. But what a shame it would be to let it languish in the prison of unrealized potential.

You can run as fast as Jesse Owens, or be a modern-day Michelangelo, if you want to. If you have the commitment and are willing to do what it takes. But it won't happen while you remain confined to your comfort zone.

As you begin to think about your definition of personal success, it's also a great opportunity to consider what legacy you want to leave behind. Do you want to be remembered as someone who played it safe or as someone who reached for the stars?

Patience: Even Greatness Must Gestate

In looking at the level of success that Sir Richard Branson, and the Virgin Group have achieved, this is no overnight success story. Along the way, there would have been many ideas and opportunities that were deemed to add value or detract from the main goal.

One of the most important aspects regarding your journey from where you are to where you choose to be is to learn and practice patience. Everything has a time and a place. There's a beginning and an end. To achieve sustainable greatness takes time.

We all know that you must have a plan and create this plan with a clear, specific goal in mind. Then you need to work your plan. Unfortunately, most entrepreneurs have ideas and dreams and think this is their plan. They are far too quick to move onto the next thing that grabs their attention—while vainly hoping everything will miraculously fall into place.

Every business owner says they are committed to their success. But all too often this is only when the waters are calm. When challenged or when something doesn't go to plan, it is far easier to cut and run. There is also the desire for instant gratification.

Declaring your BHAG is only the first step. It will only be achieved based on the effort and action that you put in. If the goal is big enough and you are inspired by it, then every day will bring forth the pieces of the jigsaw puzzle. If it becomes a chore then we suggest you go back to basics and review your goals.

We hear of amazing stories such as Branson's rock star power and credibility making it possible for Virgin Galactic to ask customers for a deposit of $20,000 for a $200,000 ticket to ride on Space Ship Two—even though it hadn't even been built. [C3:8]

At the same time, it's important to acknowledge that Branson built his brand over the course of many, many years. In 1984, coming up with such a deposit would have been out of the question, even for Branson. It has taken him a great deal of planning and an enormous amount of sweat to build the Branson brand that earns him the rewards and respect he now enjoys.

The Gestation Period

It should come as no surprise that there is no quick fix, magic wand opportunity here. It will take time and effort for you to build your own brand. There is a gestation period for great projects and great ideas; this is something that entrepreneurs, typically in a hurry, fail to understand. Gestation, of whatever variety, cannot be hurried.

No one can predict how long it will take to create your brand

and make yourself the leading authority in your field. Branson once said, "The jet stream is a very strong force, and pushing a balloon into it is like pushing up against a brick wall. But once we got into it, we found that, remarkably, the balloon went at whatever speed the wind went." [C3:9] The same is possible for you.

At times you may feel like you're pushing a wheelbarrow full of bricks up a steep hill, but one day it can all change. Your ideas and projects are living, breathing organisms, and they are fragile even after birth. Like a baby, they need patience and nurturing. The "I want it all to happen yesterday" or "are we there yet" syndromes, demonstrated so often among entrepreneurs, generally spell doom.

That said, don't confuse patience with procrastination. Procrastination means to put off doing something, such as making a decision that demands action. Procrastination is a form of irresponsibility. By contrast, patience does not mean a lack of activity and work. Patience is about your willingness to wait for results, and to keep working toward your desired goals—no matter what.

It is important for you to understand that if you do not have an existing track record or credibility in what you do, leapfrogging to stardom in your field will be unsustainable. The journey from expert to thought leader within your market has everything to do with how you think, act, and remain committed for the long term. And, as you will learn in the next chapter, it's all about who's driving your bus.

CHAPTER FOUR

INNER DIALOGUE: YOUR BIGGEST ASSET OR YOUR BIGGEST LIABILITY

It's one thing to read one of the many books about how Sir Richard Branson thinks and acts, but it's another thing altogether to actually implement his strategies. As outlined in the last chapter, the gap between most people and Richard Branson has a lot to do with having the *right* mindset.

Equally, there's another important factor to understand because this too can impede the success of small business entrepreneurs. It's called your inner dialogue. It's also commonly known as your self-talk, that little voice, or the people driving the bus.

The *bus* is a great metaphor because it depicts how influential the inner dialogue is in steering our lives. In fact, it's probably having a conversation with you right now as you read this book. The key question is: Does your inner dialogue empower you or sabotage you?

Unless you're bulletproof or living in denial, everyone has some form of self-sabotage occurring. And while we'd all love to be free of this chatter going on in our heads, it isn't about getting *rid* of it. It's about working with it. Acknowledging that it exists is the first step. Accepting it is the second step. Recognition of what's going on tends to calm those voices right down.

If you pay attention to the empowering voices, then you'll be ready to take on the world. But if you listen to the disempowering voices, you'll allow them to control you and you'll only experience a fraction of what's possible for you.

The empowering voices inspire and motivate you to take action. They put your foot firmly on the accelerator. Life becomes all about possibility and opportunity. The disempowering voices leave you frustrated, paralyzed, fearful and, quite often, even paranoid.

The key objective of those controlling little voices is getting you to stay permanently parked. If you attempt to move into the

Would you put up with a friend who day after day constantly undermined you by yelling at you? Well, isn't this what your inner dialogue is doing to you?

next gear, there will be a whole lot of noise going on about why it won't work. They'll tell you that it's only the special people who are capable of achieving great things. You'll always hear the statement, "Who do you think you are to pull *that* off?"

When you recognize that these controlling voices exist, and understand that everyone has them, is it any wonder why most small business entrepreneurs don't achieve their full potential? But as we've said, there's no point in looking for ways to get rid of your inner dialogue. It's with you for life. This is why most therapists will never be out of work.

So if you can't get rid of it, then how do you ever go from operating in the status quo to becoming the best you can be? This is what we are going to discuss next.

Personal SWOT Analysis

Most entrepreneurs at some point have invested a lot of time and energy working on their SWOT analysis—for their businesses. Just to confirm, SWOT stands for strengths, weaknesses, opportunities, and threats. It's a powerful exercise to complete for your business.

However, in this instance, we want you to consider the benefits of using this tool on yourself. We want you to gain a better understanding of who you are. Because when you're able to identify how you empower and disempower yourself, you'll gain tremendous insights and understanding into your biggest assets, along with an increased understanding of your biggest liabilities.

As an entrepreneur, and as the director of your life, it's important that you know what you're working with. I mean really know!

So here's an overview of these four key areas. We highly recommend that you schedule some time to write down your thoughts in each area. If you get stuck, e-mail us and we'll give you some extra tips. Let's get started by looking at your strengths.

Your Strengths

If you've been in business for more than twelve months, understand that your strengths will have changed. How? Why? Well, being in business is the best personal and professional development program you could ever sign up for. Every day you are stretched and you will be doing things you never thought possible.

Everyday is about thinking on your feet, making decisions on the run, and keeping the team focused, guided, directed. And then, in your spare time providing solutions to your clients.

The question is: Are you operating in a way that is congruent with your strengths? Are you doing the things in your business that you love and that inspire you? Or have you forgotten what you're truly good at?

There are many ways to identify your strengths using some of the great resources available. You can take a personal profile. You can have your team and peers complete a 360-degree analysis on you. Or you can work through this with a mentor.

When we are developing and creating a personal brand with a client, we get them to write down a list of things that other people rely on them for.

For most entrepreneurs, their technical skills are the foundations of their business—and a key reason why they started their own business. The outcome of this list is that it allows you to look at your areas of expertise, your technical skills and abilities.

This exercise establishes the first platform for your success: the foundation of your credibility. During this process, we also want to uncover your personal qualities such as your communication and leadership skills.

Too often we see that the expertise of many small business entrepreneurs is taken for granted or not recognized for it's true value. At one level, this occurs because of the negative inner dialogue. No matter how skilled, qualified, or knowledgeable you are, if your inner dialogue is driven to undermine or minimize your qualities, you will never think about promoting your talents to the world.

Work to your strengths to capitalize on all the opportunities available to you.

Let's now take a look at the area of weaknesses.

Your Weaknesses

Over the years we have had many clients who are brilliant at what they do; they are the best in their field. However, they cling to their status quo. Although they want to change, their inner dialogue is driven to protect their position. When we work with clients, it's very important to find out *who* we're dealing with—is it the client or is it their inner dialogue?

This is why, when we ask our clients to tell us what they believe their weaknesses to be, the response is, "How long have you got?" Or "How many would you like me to give you?"

No matter what your weaknesses are or how many you could list, the key is to realize they will be accentuated when your inner dialogue focuses on them. It's like the inner dialogue is on loudspeaker, drowning out all other truths about you.

Your weaknesses are, however, only the tip of the iceberg. It's important to identify what's below the surface—the factors that drive your thoughts, feelings and behaviors. This is the blind spot for most people.

As we've mentioned, many of our clients are highly skilled, qualified, and competent people. The sad thing is that they can fall into the trap of listening to the voice that says, "You're not good enough." This then translates into their conversation as: "Business is tough since the GFC," or "The clients won't pay what I'm worth," or "I can never find good people to be on my team," or "I never have enough time," or "I never seem to achieve much in a day," to name just a few. Their negative inner dialogue creates a negative reality.

The most insightful advice we give our clients is that they need to tune in, listen and acknowledge the feedback their inner dialogue gives them. However, they need to understand that they don't have to respond to or act on this advice. We encourage our clients to speak to their inner dialogue by saying, "Thanks for sharing; I'll think about that."

With all the noise going on, it's often difficult to see what opportunity lies at your feet.

Your Opportunities

We love this quote by Albert Einstein: "In the middle of difficulty lies opportunity." [C4:1] Opportunities are everywhere for you and your business. But all too often, as business owners we are too busy looking down to recognize them. The essence of a rock star mindset is about making opportunities *happen* rather than expecting, or waiting for them to happen *to you*.

For you to reach your next level, first and foremost you must be open to seeing the opportunities in your life. The second most important factor is that when opportunities do come knocking, you need to open the door and say "Yes" not "Oh, let me think about it."

There are many interpretations of the word "opportunity." Life itself is a moment-by-moment opportunity. But when life isn't going to plan, we fail to see the opportunity and default to a life of struggle.

Just to provide you with an insight into what we mean by operating in a whole world of struggle, here is a brief story about a client. The first hour of the consultation was about allowing him to download his thoughts and feelings.

I (Louise) listened to him vent his frustrations. He spoke about all the people who were to blame for his business not succeeding. I heard his justifications, his complaints, and his thoughts about how it might be easier to go get a job.

And, to be honest, this isn't the first time I've heard this type of download. This is what inspires me about coaching and mentoring entrepreneurs. Because the turning point from struggle to success is when you move the entrepreneur out of his or her own way.

Not only was it important for this client to have the space to download, but also what was required was a readjustment of his mindset. He needed to start looking at what was staring him right in his face.

The very next day this client experienced how quickly new opportunities show up. He was amazed, and like most people, not truly able to comprehend how this could have happened.

We all know that if you listen to the negative inner dialogue, it becomes a vicious downward spiral. And this is why you need to understand the power that your inner dialogue can have over you. When you focus on success—it appears. When you focus on struggle—it appears.

As an entrepreneur, one of the reasons you started your own business is because you were inspired by the possibilities. You wanted to be in the driver's seat to create, attract, and make opportunities happen. You wanted to live life from a place of choice.

However, most entrepreneurs fail to recognize that every moment they're making a choice. The key is to choose wisely. This is why it is so important to understand where you sabotage your own success.

Complete your personal SWOT analysis as a priority. Do not allow your negative inner dialogue to undermine your opportunities.

Your Threats

Most entrepreneurs consider their threats to be externally driven. And, under normal SWOT circumstances, they'd be right. However, we believe that your biggest threat is much closer than you might think.

It's not your competition, your team, your clients—nor is it your family and friends.

Have you ever stopped and thought about how *you* could be your own biggest threat? If you're like most entrepreneurs, then you might be getting in your own way.

Too often, entrepreneurs become their own worst enemy. What you create you can destroy. When you're focused, you produce results. When you become unfocused, it's chaotic and everyone suffers.

Therefore, there's no doubt that your biggest threat is your disempowering inner dialogue—especially if you treat it like your trusted friend and adviser.

Who's Driving Your Bus?
And Who is on Your Bus?

Olympic athletes don't focus their training only on physical fitness. As gold medalist Magdalena Neuner says, "I worked very hard, especially in the mental training." As quoted in an article in the Christian Science Monitor, Neuner says, "Physical fitness alone isn't sufficient. My mental training is very complex and makes me believe in myself. To control your mind is more difficult to control than your body." [C4:2]

Acknowledging your inner dialogue is important. Being able to identify the ringleader and the cohorts is critical. You need to figure out who's in charge, who is likely to block the process of change, who is judging you, who the critic is—you know—the one who waits for you to do something wrong or to fail at something new.

In some cases, this might sound like the survival of the fittest. And, it is. However, once you know who's on the bus, then the real work can begin. You'll be able to identify the nuances of your inner dialogue and take control of your decisions. That, in turn, will have a positive impact on your business and your life.

The real opportunity for you is to get into the driver's seat. Then ensure that your passengers are in the right seats for the right roles. Once you put your foot firmly on the accelerator and you're flat out having fun, the inner dialogue tends to become very quiet.

Always remember: It's your life and you deserve to shine.

Learning to Be Unreasonable

By conducting a SWOT analysis on yourself, two things are possible. The first is that you'll put the spotlight on your disempowering self-talk. You'll recognize the negativity, the burdens, the inadequacies, and the frustrations associated with running a business and taking yourself to the next level.

The second insight you'll discover is that there are some very empowering and wise voices—waiting to be heard. The wise voices represent the spirit of Branson—the courageous, inspiring, go-getting souls that want you to succeed.

These are the voices of encouragement you heard when you first went into business. These are the voices you heard when you got your first client or big deal. These are the voices that speak to you about how brilliant you really are, and about what you're here to do with your life. They are often, quietly spoken. However, when you're open to listening they will be very clear, very uplifting and extremely encouraging.

So you have a choice. You can continue to focus on your past and concentrate on what hasn't gone well—while beating yourself up about where you've struggled. Or you can begin the journey of learning to be unreasonable—and in action. This is the spirit of Sir Richard Branson that we most admire.

For everything he has achieved, we have no doubt that he had a little voice telling him he couldn't do it and shouldn't do it. But he went after it anyway. You have a choice. Begin to live courageously like Branson—because you might just surprise yourself about what you're capable of achieving.

Being unreasonable is easier than you think. What we mean by "being unreasonable" is to live in a way that runs counter to the logic of your negative inner dialogue. Negative thoughts have a logic to them that can be very powerful, even though false. The key is to oppose that negative logic.

Your positive ideas and actions don't need to be earth shattering or totally out of the box. It could be as simple as getting up half an hour earlier to go for a walk, to have a good breakfast before work, or to call five clients just to stay in touch with them. It might be saying thank you to your team.

To help you get started, here is a tip.

At the end of the day, write down ten things you achieved that you think were unreasonable actions. Then write down ten things that you did that were enjoyable and fun. Take baby steps—begin by focusing on the little wins and pay attention to the power of writing them down.

When our clients do this exercise, they very quickly see how their empowering voices become more prominent. It's all about consciously reprogramming your mind. It does take practice, but the impact on your business and your life will far outweigh the effort required.

An Unreasonable Mentor

When your inner voice gets louder, this is when you need access to an unreasonable mentor. The definition of an unreasonable mentor is someone who can listen to what you're saying, relate to and have first-hand personal experience but doesn't buy into your pity party.

After allowing you the time and space to download, their role is to ensure that you don't revert to business as usual. It's about pushing through and gaining your next insight into who you are.

No one can survive alone. An aspect of creating your BHAG, and learning to practice patience, is also about knowing when to ask for help.

All great rock stars are surrounded by other great musicians, as well as all the people involved in marketing, setting up concerts, and recording. Even with all his success, Branson never fails to bring in the assistance of experts. Asking for help is not a weakness. It takes courage to say, "I don't know it all and could use some advice."

Getting a qualified mentor helps hold you to the commitments you make to yourself. You will have to check-in with someone else about the steps you're taking toward your goals. A mentor can also serve as a sounding board for the ideas and plans you are gestating.

Business is a team sport—it's never a one-man band. Richard Branson always makes a point of acknowledging the people who helped him along the way. And, it is well known that one of his most special collaborators was Sir Freddie Laker, the original business rebel. Branson describes him as his personal hero and mentor—perhaps he was his own Yoda.

Choose the Right Mentor for the Right Reason

There are a couple of points worth noting about mentors.

The first is the importance of having the right mentors and role models. If your heart is set on boosting your sales and building your brand by becoming an authority in your field, then get the right mentor. Don't choose just any mentor. You need someone who has walked, and continues to walk, a path similar to yours.

The second point is: Don't fall into the classic trap of the blind leading the blind. Ask this simple question when interviewing a prospective consultant, coach or mentor: "Do you have first-hand experience in the area for which I seek counsel and mentoring?" If not, find someone who has.

The power of connecting with the right mentor is so aptly described in the following story about Sir Freddie Laker and Sir Richard Branson.

A World War II Royal Air Force veteran, Laker invented the low-cost, long-haul airline, launching Laker SkyTrain in 1977. Flying from London's Gatwick to New York, the airline was the forerunner of Virgin Airlines. In 1984, a young Branson decided to take up Laker's original license between Gatwick and New York and started an airline called Virgin Atlantic. The rest is history. Without Laker's efforts, we would never be enjoying affordable air travel as we do today. So thank you, Sir Freddie. [C4:3]

The Golden Buddha

The key to creating your personal brand begins with valuing yourself and, from that perspective, being willing to do what's required. If you are not willing to do whatever it takes or to go the extra mile, then no one can help you.

If you're not ready to value yourself, then go back to the drawing board. Examine the mindset you're in. And regardless of what that is, remember that you already have what it takes to be an outrageous success. It's a case of rediscovering your own inner greatness.

In 1957, when a plaster statue of Buddha, that was thought to have little value, was being moved to a new temple in Bangkok, a cable broke and the statue fell into the mud—an event seen as a bad omen by the workers. They ran away, leaving the statue in the mud covered only with a rug. As if to confirm their fears, a storm hammered throughout the night, flooding the entire city.

At dawn the next day, a temple monk who had dreamed that the statue was divinely inspired went to see the fallen Buddha image. Shining a lamp on the rug, he saw a glint of yellow reflecting back at him. On examination, he found that the overnight rain had melted the plaster.

Gradually removing the gooey mess, he discovered the statue was made of solid gold. To hide its value, it had been covered in plaster two centuries earlier, when the Burmese were about to sack the city. Modern people thought it was only a plaster statue.[C4:4]

The moral of this story is that *you* are like the golden Buddha. Your self-limiting beliefs are the plaster that stops your authentic self from shining. Know that your "greatness lives on the edge of destruction"—destruction of your negative self-beliefs.

Don't be like the construction workers, jumping to wrong conclusions because they only looked at what was on the surface. Don't focus on what is not working in your life or on how difficult your dreams have been to accomplish. Don't accept a limited definition of yourself.

Find the gold that's underneath the plaster. Unless you decide to own your true magnificence, you will never discover all that you can be. And, the world needs your unique and extraordinary talents.

By becoming an authority in your field, you can prosper and help many others within your sphere of influence prosper with you. It all starts with you. You can choose to boldly display your greatness to the world and reach beyond your current limits. No matter what you decide, always know that you get to choose.

In the next chapter, we will focus on another of the factors that most prevents entrepreneurs from achieving their full potential: fear. Overcoming your fear is crucial as you develop your personal brand and establish yourself as the leading expert in your field.

CHAPTER FIVE

BEING UNSTOPPABLE IN THE FACE OF FEAR

Fear shows up for people in many different ways. It can show up when we are moving into unknown territory, faced with a life altering decision, feeling threatened by something or, in an extreme case, when death comes knocking at our door!

Entrepreneurs often experience a nagging sense of fear of failure. But they can be equally fearful of success. Fear will usually show up when you're about to take on something meaningful.

As an entrepreneur, you have two choices. You can choose to be stopped by fear—allow fear to consume your spirit, your courage, and all the things you stand for. Or you can choose to become unstoppable in the face of fear: meaning, allow fear to drive you, inspire you, propel you and move you forward.

Choosing to become a business rock star is a decision that will undoubtedly force you out of your comfort zone. However, you won't die as a result of this decision. In fact, it's probably far more frightening to consider becoming a powerful human being—someone who could become an outrageous success.

It's a given that when you set great, big, audacious goals, you will come face-to-face with your fears. If it's something that you've never done before—you will immediately be pushed out of your comfort zone and enter into uncharted waters. And although you know the destination, you will have no way of predicting what lies ahead.

Fear is a Natural Part of the Process

Now, don't get us wrong. We can assure you that developing a personal brand will be a fun and exciting adventure. However, it's a journey that will require you to learn how to embrace your fears and concerns. Being able to recognize fear, and use it to propel yourself forward is far better than allowing it to destroy you and your business.

Personal branding is not a popularity contest. Nor is it an opportunity for a boost of ego. Personal branding is about stepping up, being bold, and being proud of your greatness. Yes, your goal can be outrageous, but in order to have it be successful, it must be commercially sound. You have to be willing to take risks—risks you would normally never dream of taking.

When you move out of your comfort zone it can be quite overwhelming—it can make you feel anxious or plain terrified! We've seen otherwise rational business owners become immobilized by fear. Some perceive the very people who want them to succeed as being the enemy. Fear often leads them to criticize the very people who support them. The people who are on the receiving end of this criticism are often their biggest fans. So fear not only paralyzes, it can also alienate you from your entire support network. This human reaction is referred to as fight or flight response—a term coined by physiologist Walter Cannon.

With this in mind, let's take a look at some strategies to help you overcome your fears.

Fear Resides in Your Interpretation

The harsh reality is that fear will always exist somewhere in your life. It will never go away. It simply cannot be eliminated.

In today's world, we are taught or conditioned to be fearful. We are flooded with media that tells us that the world we live in is dangerous. We are told stories of murder, abuse, war, natural disasters, and there is very little—if any—news that really inspires and empowers us. Good news does not sell newspapers, but disasters, conflicts, violence, and other mayhem always attracts an audience.

Is it any wonder that our thoughts drift to "anything I build on could go pear-shaped?"

However, the great news is that there is a far more powerful way of doing life. Fear doesn't have to immobilize us. Life can be grand and extraordinary. Life can teach us. Because life is, after all, a learning experience. And, while it doesn't get any easier, how we approach life, and how we integrate our lessons, is the difference that will make the difference.

Do you remember what it was like in school? Every year the lessons became a little more challenging. As adults we somehow don't expect the challenges to keep coming. However, this is always when we do our best work—when we're being stretched and when we break through to another layer.

Opportunities show up, we grow our skills and build on our talents. We become stronger and our confidence expands.

Overcoming challenges is an integral part of our evolution as human beings.

The key is to turn your fears into a positive experience. When you think about them rationally and think of them as a way to evolve, the experience becomes exciting and worthwhile.

Fear can be a thrilling experience when we let ourselves enjoy it. Remember when you spent a day at the fun park taking a ride on the big roller coaster, screaming your head off while riding a flying fox, or bungee jumping? Remember the adrenalin pulsing through you as you rode kayaks through the

What do you see? Do you see the face of an old lady or a young woman?
It all depends on what you focus on.
Focus on fear and you will see all the evidence you need to be fearful.

rapids or conquered your first parachute jump?

If you allow yourself to be paralyzed with fear and never take the leap, you'll be destined to stay stuck where you are and always wonder "What if?"

The question is: Would it not be empowering to partner up with fear and have it be your new best friend, supporting you and helping you grow on your journey?

As you make this choice, the place to focus is not on what is actually happening—but on how you're interpreting it.

Separate Facts from Emotions

The human psyche, as we know, is intricately complex and highly intelligent. Therefore, one would expect, that we mere mortals could easily make a distinction between what is real versus what is not.

Wrong. Human beings have mastery in being able to complicate the most simple of things.

So, in the context of fear, what is real? Put simply—that which is fact. And, what isn't real is what you make fear mean.

Fear exists. We aren't challenging this. However, what we are challenging is the driving force behind the meaning that human beings attach to fear, and then allowing that to steer them to success or failure.

Rather than acknowledging it is there and working with it in a powerful way, we buy into it. We allow it to dictate our life, spend years believing it, and then wake up one day wondering what we have done with our life.

The key to working with your fear is about identifying and acknowledging its existence, and most importantly, not allowing yourself to become blocked by it.

Let's take the example of you becoming a published author. (We've chosen this illustration because, as we will show in a later chapter, writing a book can be an integral part of your personal brand.)

> *The facts: What is real?* *Writing a book will showcase your level of expertise and knowledge, and position you as the authority in your professional niche.*
>
> *Your possible emotional response:* *Others might ask, "Who do you think you are?" or you fear facing ridicule for even thinking about writing a book.*

These are classic emotions at work. Sigmund Freud described these emotional responses as the awakening of the unconscious mind, and it is these emotions that can regulate what the entrepreneur experiences as "reality."

The mind is the most powerful hard drive we'll ever operate. Edward de Bono, father of lateral thinking, stated that the brain is a filing cabinet. Scientists describe the brain as an automated warehouse of multisensory records of successive moments (memory records).

It is for these reasons that most elite athletes use a basic mind training system in order to master the mental skills needed to consistently perform at their best. These athletes win their races in their minds before they even get to the start line. They program their mind with positive images.

By contrast, dwelling on your fears will program your mind in a negative way. If you tend to react this way it is because, based on the images in your memory banks, you are creating images of what can go wrong. Then, like most people, you will run mental replays of these images.

Continuing with the example of becoming a published author, to separate facts from emotions, you need to ask four specific questions.

Question 1: What's your viewpoint?

Look at yourself and be honest about your feelings. Remember there are no right or wrong responses. Write down what you think and feel. If you think you can't back up your claims then accept that. If you think your competitors are going to use this opportunity to put the boot in your ribs, then that is real for you too. Acknowledge that this is how you feel. The important thing is to clearly establish what you think about the idea.

Before we published our first book, we believed that we weren't credible enough to do so under our own banner. And guess what? We were absolutely right. Although a blind spot for us, the way we were operating gathered evidence to support this belief.

Thankfully, we had a great support structure around us, people who were willing to stand up for us, and who encouraged us to become authors. If we weren't open to viewpoints different to our own, we'd have been forever stuck with the notion that we were not good enough. And this book, our third, wouldn't have been a possibility.

Never underestimate that your mind is the key to making your hopes and dreams a reality.

Question 2: What evidence do you have that supports your viewpoint?

Writing down the evidence that supports your viewpoint will allow you to clearly see what you think the weaknesses are in your plan. If you really think that people around you would question your ability or your right to be an authority in your profession, then write down any evidence you see of that happening.

If you think that your competitors are going to erode your credibility, write down how you think that might happen. Whatever your fear is, you can determine if there really is any evidence to substantiate your perspective. And if there is, you'll be able to address the facts in a positive way. The very first step is to get your thoughts written down, on paper, and out of your head.

Question 3: What are your thoughts, feelings, and emotions when you are fearful?

Be willing to admit your fear. If you are scared or anxious, know that it serves absolutely no purpose to suffer in silence. Whether you talk to your spouse, a business coach, or trusted adviser, the fact is that simply getting things off your chest can relieve a lot of fear.

Keeping your feelings to yourself will magnify danger and vulnerability while minimizing your sense of competence. In other words it reflects the acronym for fear: Fantasy Expectations Appearing Real.

Your thoughts, feelings, and emotions are a reflection of your inner state of mind. That's why it's so important to acknowledge them. If you don't, it could result in physical symptoms such as being unable to sleep or feeling like you're spinning out of control. By being aware of your emotions, you can take responsibility for dealing with your fears.

When you talk yourself into becoming fearful, it's a vicious cycle and takes you further into the depths of despair.

Question 4: Who could you become if you were free of fearful thoughts?
This is a very powerful question: it could transform the way you approach life and your business.

To answer it, you need to step out of your own skin and see what is possible. Always remember that people such as Richard Branson are no different than you? Branson is an ordinary person following his heart. Stop being yourself for a moment—with all your fears—and consider what life would be like if you were free from their constraints.

When you think negative thoughts you can turn that into a self-fulfilling prophecy and vice-versa. So wouldn't it be better to fill your mind with positive thoughts?

Six Steps to Overcoming Fear

No matter how well prepared you are, setting a goal beyond your comfort zone and moving into action will generate varying degrees of fear. In addition to what we've already discussed, we believe the following six steps will help you live beyond your fears so that you can accomplish your goals.

Step One: Faith

Faith is the flipside of fear. It is often said that fear manifests itself when you are faced with the unknown. However, the unknown future is a clean slate. If we project the anticipation of dreaded consequences into our future, then we can only but feel afraid.

Faith, on the other hand, is an inherent attribute of the human soul. We're not talking about blind faith. It's about knowing in your heart that what you're setting out to achieve is absolutely possible without you having proof or physical evidence just yet.

If you have faith in your ability to become a business rock

star, then train your mind to focus on becoming exactly that.

When an entrepreneur is operating from fear, this notion of faith can be difficult to grasp, and it is very reasonable to ask for proof and evidence. But when you feel like you are taking a big leap into the unknown, you do have to rely on an element of faith. They don't call it a leap of faith for nothing!

The reality is that you're never going to know every possible scenario, every single risk or every single opportunity that will come your way. No human being has that kind of knowledge. So we operate by venturing into the unknown at many points of our life—and that's when we need to rely on faith.

If you reconnect with the faith that you had when you first started your business you'll realize that you didn't know if your business was going to succeed. You didn't know if it would still be operating the way it is today. You had that faith once. Just draw on it again. Step out of your comfort zone and draw on the strength you know is already within you.

Step Two: Your Deadline

If you get into a flap when you set big goals, then simply adjust your deadline. Structure your business so you can dedicate time for working on your new plan and personal brand. Be willing to adjust your deadline so it produces less stress.

Now, just a word of warning: Don't get into the habit of continually moving this deadline. Remember that moving it too often can just be procrastination. So if you move it once make sure the new deadline you set is realistic and reasonable, then stick to it relentlessly.

If you're working with a business coach, his or her job is to help you by being an unreasonable friend. Ideally, the coach's role is to stretch you and make you accountable to your plan. Rely on someone to help you stay accountable, just as Edmund Hillary and Tenzing Norgay relied on each other to reach the summit of Mount Everest.

We're sure there were many moments when either of them expressed their concerns or fears, but they had each other for support. And always ensure that you find the right person to support you and hold you accountable to your goal.

Step Three: Make Fear Your Priority

To overcome fear, the solution is not to avoid it, but to face it. To stare it down. By being aware of your fear you'll help to dissolve it. Let's say you're worried about how your clients will react if you spend time working on a book while your customer service is not up to par.

To overcome this fear, don't avoid it or suppress it. Instead, acknowledge exactly what you're scared of. Make it a priority. Put it front and center so you can deal with it and, ultimately, you will find solutions to get over it for good.

Admitting that you are afraid is easier said than done. Another way to lose the grip that fear has on you is to tell the truth: that you are, in fact, fearful. Always remember that the truth will set you free.

Step Four: Find An Expert Mentor

We have already discussed the importance of having a great mentor, someone who will be your unreasonable friend. Ideally they need to be in the mold of Sir Freddie, the mentor for Richard Branson. You need a proven expert who has been there and done that.

Step Five: Reinforce Positive Thoughts with Simple Techniques

It is easier to focus on the negative than the positive. We tend to analyze and examine the negative thoughts, but all to no avail. The result is that you will spiral downwards. One way to break the cycle is to notice the negative thought patterns, and choose something that is positive and uplifting, something that will lead to positive and beneficial results.

We know this is easier said than done. However, there are some actions you can take to make it easier. One methodology is through auto-suggestion or self-hypnosis that is directed to the subconscious mind. Such techniques directly program your mind with affirmations and suggestions that are in line with your goals. You can use this programming as an effective method to also reduce stress and induce relaxation.

Once you are familiar with this technique, it's an extremely simple tool anyone can use effectively; you can be completely in control of what you put into your mind when you are in a suggestible state. This state is known as *Alpha*. It is defined as an altered state of consciousness, as opposed to *Beta*, which is considered to be a fully conscious state. When you are in the *Alpha* state you can insert positive suggestions in your mind.

Here is a simple process to program your mind with positive suggestions. First you must get in touch with your fear. To relieve the fear, please follow these instructions.

Sit in a place where you are comfortable and will not be disturbed for five minutes. Uncross your legs and hands and close your eyes. Take a few deep breaths and relax.

Now, ask yourself the following questions:

"What am I fearful of?"

"What physical sensations are associated to my fear?"

If your throat is dry, then visualize your throat moistening. If your palms are hot and sweaty then visualize a cool breeze cooling that part of your body. See your body actually relax. Now see yourself asking and then receiving the positive outcomes you desire.

This simple five-minute process will relax you even during

the busiest day and return you to a calmer state.

For some people, meditation is useful in quieting the mind and identifying your fears. Connecting with your thoughts will help you consider fear in a more rational way. You'll be operating with measured actions instead of reacting with knee jerk impulses.

We recommend meditation, and there are many techniques available. You just need to find the methodology that suits you.

Step Six: Don't Get Attached to the Outcome

Observing Branson, one cannot fail to note that the man is not attached to the outcome. He just stays focused on playing full out, being in action, rather than getting attached to the problem of whether or not he will have a successful outcome.

This does not mean he doesn't care about the results. On the contrary, he sets the intention and then plays full-out to reach his goal. Someone playing full-out doesn't have time to get attached to what others might be thinking. Their focus is on their commitment, and on doing what they said they'd do.

To Be or Not to Be

After all is said and done, you have the choice to stay in your comfort zone or to make a conscious decision to rise above that reality. It takes courage to say: "I am going to bring out my inner Branson and become an authority in my niche."

The famous British playwright George Bernard Shaw once said: "A reasonable man adapts himself to his environment. An unreasonable man persists in attempting to adapt his environment to suit himself. Therefore, all progress depends on the unreasonable man." C5:1

You may have to face the truth about whether fear is keeping you where you are. Or as Hamlet once asked: "To be or not to be. That is the question." C5:2

Refusing to align your life according to the rules dictated by your fear, and then stepping into a life dictated by your own conscience is a weighty choice—one not to be taken lightly but one that will make you feel lighter.

You will feel lighter because you will be free—free from the control of your fears and free to live a life aligned with your true identity. You'll sense that a burden has been lifted and that the world appears to you in a new light. And that new freedom will have a radical impact on your business.

In the next chapter we take a look at the topic of how to deal with problems and challenges and finding a problem that is worthy of your efforts. Too often the entrepreneur is bogged down with small-time problems that are designed to distract, frustrate, and take you away from what you're capable of.

What we want you to consider is creating problems that challenge you to discover your greatness and realize your true potential.

CHAPTER SIX

PROBLEMS WORTHY OF BRANSON

Most entrepreneurs are extremely positive and highly optimistic. However, every now and again, they can become trapped in a pity party attitude and the world around them looks and feels like a glass half empty. This may sound dramatic, but when an entrepreneur falls into this paradigm, the dialogue is all about what's not working.

We hear statements such as "life is a series of problems that flow one after another." "It's hard out there," and "Things seem to be getting tougher for small business owners year after year." Life can appear tough—no matter what we are doing. Business, like everything else, has its share of problems. A lot of people don't understand just how stressful the business world can be. And although your family and friends might think you're some sort of superman or superwoman for doing what you do, they probably don't grasp the burden that rests on your shoulders.

We understand that you have to keep the business afloat, not just for your pride but because people depend on you— including your family, employees and your customers. They can't see that you are drowning in responsibilities and that uncertainty lurks around every corner.

While we can all try to camouflage our problems by calling them "challenges," at the end of the day they can feel like a massive pain in the butt.

If this is where you're at in regards to your business and your life, you're probably thinking "why would I want to take on another level of responsibility."

And, you'd be right. However, when we take on a problem that is way bigger than the general day-to-day issues, we become highly creative and innovative in our thinking.

Our Problems Can Improve Our Business

Richard Branson has certainly demonstrated to the world how to treat problems as opportunities and allow them to improve the way we do business. In choosing to operate with this mindset, you also choose to assume full responsibility for the direction of your life.

I (William) finally learned this important lesson. While it may look like I made a radical decision, it was a way of stepping outside the disempowering context in which I was stuck. My new identity liberated me from my past and channeled me down a far more empowering current.

What you need to ask yourself is this: Are you willing to see your problems as worthy of your attention and as a chance for personal growth, or will you see them as a ball and chain that will drag you to the bottom of the ocean?

Some people resign themselves to this way of seeing problems but others put them to good use. Learning to make a positive choice is an essential skill to develop, and one that will really empower you.

You might have been told, or you may simply believe, that if you set a big goal it will become an added burden that you just don't need. And who needs another thing to worry about?

However, all your inevitable hurdles in life should not keep you from striving to improve your business. Nor should your current challenges get in the way of developing a strong personal brand. Problems are no different than your fears. When you stop long enough to identify what the source of the problem is, you can then find the appropriate solution.

Running a small business is never about getting everything perfect. Consider that all your past hurdles, obstacles, and challenges felt overwhelming and daunting at the time. However, entrepreneurs thrive on challenges. And the bigger the challenge, the greater the opportunity.

The Branson Approach to Problems

This is another wonderful quote from George Bernard Shaw: "I want to be thoroughly used up when I die, for the harder I work the more I live. I rejoice in life for its own sake." [C6:1] Could there be a better way to describe people like Richard Branson, Martha Stewart, or Steve Jobs?

In Branson's case, he rejoices in life not by ignoring his problems, but by realizing that to become the person he truly is, to align himself with his core values, he had to take on extreme challenges. We acknowledge that this is in his nature. For him, it is all about seeing life as an adventure and possibility.

Branson's success arises from his relentless eagerness for taking on problems worthy of his character. Even though he

When you are living your life to the fullest and doing what you love, you are energized and excited about what's possible. When you are not, then life is just a struggle. You have the power to choose.

has reached a high level of success, he simply ups the ante and starts setting even more extraordinary personal challenges. His appetite for self-empowerment knows no bounds.

It is not as though these challenges made life easier for him. The entire point of setting these challenges for himself was to make life a little bit harder so that he had to step up to the plate and see what he was made of. The lesson to be learned from Branson is to use our problems as catalysts for success.

Transcend Your Problems by Creating a Bigger Problem

Throughout this book we have discussed the concept of the BHAG and how *every* entrepreneur would benefit from having one. The reason we are stressing this is that it will provide you with a problem worthy of your efforts.

Imagine living a life where you took on something so big, so audacious that you had to pinch yourself every day due to the synchronicity that was occurring in your life. Imagine the joy, the pleasure, and the excitement of stretching your brain to seek solutions to a worthwhile problem. Imagine transcending the tiny little ankle biting problems that you're currently dealing with.

Over the last twenty years of coaching and mentoring entrepreneurs, we have found that they can get caught up in minor and inconsequential problems. And to their own detriment they use small problems to distract them from stepping up and taking on something big and ambitious. It's far too easy to get involved and be the one that resolves the problems. However, at the end of the day it really is a waste of their talents.

This is why we constantly remind our clients that the issue is not that they have these small problems. Such problems are part and parcel of life. The real issue is that they don't have a problem that's big enough to be worthy of who they are.

A Little White Ball and a Fast Car

Let's look at the metaphor of games. The world is full of games; all involve a problem or challenge that must be overcome in order to win. Some are likely to be exciting to you while others are not. It all boils down to the type of games that are worthy of your attention, time, resources, and energy. This is the key to understanding the nature of problems.

For example, let us look briefly at golf and Formula One racing. Both involve big money and hundreds of millions of fans all over the world. When you get down to it, the essence of golf is about someone hitting a little white ball into a hole using a metal stick. It sounds so simple on paper, and yet the skill required to be a professional golfer is so high that they are rewarded with massive prize money.

Formula One car racing is not much different than golf. You drive an extremely fast car around and around a track to the sounds of cheering fans and not much happens for hours until the final moments when everyone scrambles to overtake the leader in order to cross the finish line first.

In both cases what happens is that people agree on a set of rules and declare certain elements of the game to be very important. The amazing thing is that everyone agrees with the rules and takes them seriously, until someone comes along and challenges the rules.

In his own way, this is exactly what Branson did. Even though bringing change created new problems, the problems were worthy of his time and effort. And we're not talking about creating problems just for the sake of some excitement and drama so you can ride in on your white horse and save the day. We're talking about creating a problem that brings out the best in you.

From Self-Doubt to Empowerment

At some point or another, we all question what we are doing with our life. This is natural. As Branson, in his book *Losing my Virginity*, said, "I'd seemed to have run out of a purpose in my life. I'd proved myself to myself in many areas. I'd just turned forty. I was seeking a new challenge. I was even considering selling up." C6:2

So even great people can face times of self-doubt. But the difference is that they use these moments to propel themselves further in their pursuit of success. They do this by not letting themselves off the hook. We all have a tendency to make excuses in our business or personal lives. This is so common that we often forget we are doing it!

We all know how it goes. We say, "I can't take the risk at the moment because I have a family to look after," or "I can't do it now because money is tight." These are things we tell ourselves to make sure we don't take the leap into the unknown. But the fact is, there will *never* be a perfect time to take a leap.

When we think about what Branson has done, it becomes

clear that he was never foolish enough to believe there would be no problems; rather, he realized that if he were aware of the problems, he could use them to his advantage.

At some point you just have to make the leap into the unknown. There is no promise that it will all work out, or that your problems will disappear. But your new problems will at least be problems worthy of your character. They will be your *own* problems and that, after all, was the point of becoming your own boss.

If you want to grow, then you have to step outside your safe boundaries. It is outside your comfort zone that you become a greater person because it is there that the really difficult challenges (and rewards) reside. Nobody ever hears about the millionaire who became rich by playing it safe.

Our entire culture is based around the idea that problems shouldn't exist, but this is a pipe dream. There will always be problems and instead of trying to somehow eliminate them, the much smarter option is to find a problem that is worthy of both your time and your energy.

When you find this kind of problem you will see a marked improvement in your determination and focus. There is nothing like a good challenge to get the forces of a determined character flowing! A worthy problem will propel you forward, drive you and excite you. An unworthy problem will keep you stuck in a downward spiral of negativity.

That's why it's important to pay close attention to your choices during the times when you question yourself. It's during these moments that you often have a chance to choose the problems that are significant and worthy of your character. It's a time when you have a chance to evaluate your goals and perhaps create a new and better one. In a sense, this is what developing a personal brand is all about.

The Focus of Athletes

It's remarkable to see how great athletes choose a positive, empowering context that enables them to embrace problems with tenacity and focus. We all recognize that there is something special about great athletes, but it's hard to pin down the precise qualities that make them unique. Why is this so? After all, they're only human, even though at times we consider them to be superhuman!

Perhaps what separates professional athletes from the rest of us is their unique ability to remain determined and focused even when their long-term goals are years down the line. Take Tiger Woods, who started playing golf as a child. Instead of hanging out with his friends, he was driven by being the best golfer in the world.

Develop your BHAG muscle.

For some, this level of determined focus may seem rare. It isn't. And the reason it exists is because people like Woods do what they do because they have an unwavering passion and commitment.

Magic Johnson, one of the all-time basketball greats, once said, "I am a businessman. This is what I do each and every day. I love it. I love coming to work. I never have a bad day." [C6:3] This is the kind of attitude that makes all the difference.

A long-term, passionate commitment to a BHAG is crucial as you begin to develop your personal brand. Taking on any kind of challenge will bring with it its own set of problems.

For his part, Richard Branson can take on his big audacious goals because he has developed his "BHAG muscles." But he developed them over a long time. By creating your very own BHAG, you'll begin the process of developing your own muscle. It's no different to when you first go to the gym—there's a beginners level and there's an advanced level.

Have you ever noticed that when people first go to the gym, they spend a lot of time comparing themselves to the people doing the heavy lifting? However, the people who can lift the heavy weights are focused, which is the reason they got where they are in the first place.

What's important is that you don't spend your time comparing yourself to others who are doing heavy lifting. You need to do your own thing. You can learn from them and ask them about where they get their focus and determination, but never let yourself be dissuaded from your own tasks by focusing on what others are doing. This is a classic case of how you can sabotage your success.

When you start to think positively, the world looks different. The problems of each day become unique challenges that make you a better and stronger person. This is how professional athletes see the world. They know that they need to do so many laps of the field or so many push-ups and they also know that tomorrow they will pay the price in pain. But they do it anyway.

They do it because they have learned to see their problems as catalysts for something bigger, and as a way to propel themselves to greatness. This is why we are always in awe of their achievements.

Always Aim High

Just as we can learn a lot from professional athletes, we can also learn a lot from Branson when it comes to combining a fierce determination with a passion for your business.

Branson says: "You don't learn to walk by following rules. You learn by doing, and by falling over." [C6:4] In other words, it's guaranteed that you will make mistakes by taking a step out of your comfort zone, but this is the most natural thing in the world. Once again, this is how we evolve as human beings. If you are going to fall over, it may as well be in the service of something great.

There is no reason not to aim high. Just remember: it all begins by finding a problem that challenges you to discover your true potential.

By developing a personal brand, by living in alignment with who you are, and by having a BHAG, you will enjoy facing problems that really matter to you. And there is no doubt that when entrepreneurs are striving to achieve their big hairy audacious goals, there is a much more positive energy flowing in their life. And when you are willing to create goals that inspire you to greatness, others will be inspired by your achievements.

Our next chapter looks at the importance of being an inspiring entrepreneur and how to achieve this.

CHAPTER SEVEN

BE INSPIRING

Sir Richard Branson is an inspiration to people from all walks of life. Unique among business leaders, entrepreneurs, celebrities, and rock stars alike, he channels this inspiration through his business and his brand.

It's easy to be inspired by Richard Branson, not just because of what he has and continues to achieve, but because of the way he goes about business and life with *unlimited* energy and his own brand of cheeky irreverence. After all, who else would say: "I'm a bit like the Queen in that I don't carry much cash?" *C7:1*

There has always been, and always will be, people who inspire us and make their presence felt. In today's highly connected world, it's very easy to rattle off an endless list of inspirational leaders, artists, scientists, thinkers and entrepreneurs who are in the same vein. People such as Nelson Mandela, Oprah Winfrey, Will Smith, Michael Jordan, Mother Theresa or Steve Jobs, just to name a few.

It's as though some common thread links them all–almost as if they were tapping into a single source for their inspiration and success. And maybe they are. Your ability to learn from inspiring leaders is what will assist you in developing your own personal brand.

So, in the case of Sir Richard Branson, what is the source of his inspiration? Some would say it's his personality. Some would say it's his attitude. Others might conclude it's all about his mindset. Perhaps it's in his genes. Or maybe it's the people he associates with. It could also be learned behavior rather than instinctive. And without a doubt it will be the alchemy of all of the above.

But let's focus on you. If we were to speak with your business colleagues, clients, employees, family, and friends, how might they describe you? Some are likely to say that you've done really well in your business—going from a start up business to becoming a reasonably sized company. Perhaps they see you as the expert in your chosen industry, the go-to person when they need your product or advice.

Some of your colleagues in certain circles may go so far as to mention your name and have people easily recognize you for what you do. Others might describe you as a rock star because in their eyes who you are, what you do, and how you make things happen is inspiring.

However, the key question is: How do you see yourself? Do you believe you are inspiring? Do you consider yourself to be an expert? Or do you believe that the inspirational trait is bestowed only upon a privileged few high fliers, such as Richard Branson?

We've specifically designed this chapter to show you how you can be a person who inspires others, but without creating a false image of yourself and your company. We will do so by addressing two important questions: How does a person become someone who can inspire others and why this is important for developing a brand?

Living a Life of Endless Possibilities

People who inspire us do not go about their day saying, "Today I am going to inspire someone." In fact to the contrary, they are usually very humble. There is a quiet confidence about them. And there is often a magnetic energy that you feel very drawn to.

As entrepreneurs, when we have the good fortune to connect with inspiring people, whether this is personally, or through hearing or reading about them, we are touched in a way that is often unexplainable. It's a feeling—a knowingness that you are in the presence of a special human being. You might have experienced a tingling sensation on your skin, or found yourself moved to tears by what they are saying or doing.

People who inspire us open our hearts and minds to what's truly possible. And as we've said, it's easy to be inspired by Sir Richard Branson because there are many aspects of his business and his life to be inspired by.

For instance, his achievements in business, the way he has gone about setting up and expanding the Virgin Group. From a personal perspective, there's his sense of humor, that amazing smile, and his ongoing desire for adventure and fun. From a leadership and social responsibility perspective, he also inspires leaders from all walks of life to get behind the big issues of our times, in particular the concerns for the planet.

And what remains constant is his desire to connect, support, give back, and encourage entrepreneurs to shine as can be seen from Branson's quote: "Entrepreneurs are the life blood of major economies and can help create thriving communities that in turn generate jobs." [C7:2]

Certainly, these are factors that make him an inspiration, but deeper still is the fact that Branson's life can be summed up by Helen Keller's quote: "Life is either a daring adventure or nothing." [C7:3]

He sees life as an endless list of possibilities. He thinks big and he refuses to play it safe.

In short, Branson is not interested in merely being realistic. He lives outside the box of realism and pursues possibilities and big dreams.

Being realistic is not a default virtue, as some would have you believe. Rather, it is the most commonly travelled road to mediocrity. Just imagine if you were someone who is rigidly realistic or someone who views life as nothing more than a struggle. How inspirational would you be?

Being inspiring is about thinking of the possibilities that you can create, not about being hampered by notions of realism. It's about being willing to constantly ask yourself "What if?" questions. And know that it takes the same amount of time and energy to ask positive "What if?" questions as it takes to perpetually contemplate problems and obstacles. In fact, thinking realistically is usually a lot harder because it feels like you have one foot on the brake and the other on the accelerator.

Becoming an inspiring leader for your business goes beyond "thinking" like an inspiring leader. It requires you to step up and *be* an inspiring leader. And we've already said that you are an inspiration.

The Invisible Branson is about the "inner game," the mindset required to develop a successful and sustainable brand. Richard Branson is a unique and inspiring entrepreneur, and we believe that you too have these qualities within you; they're just waiting to be unleashed.

Be Inspired by Your Goals

For you to be inspirational, you must be inspired by your own goals. As we've said, the starting point is to ask "What if?" questions and to create a project or a goal that would, first and foremost, inspire *you*. If you are not inspired by your own goals, then there is no way that your life will inspire others.

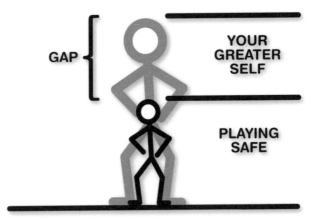

When you realize that you are the source and the spirit of your goals,
you bridge the gap between your physical self and your greater self.

You are the source and the spirit of your goal—its veritable essence. And whether *you* realize this or not, you need to trust that you have the qualities needed to become an inspiring leader. In fact, every human being is blessed with the inspirational gene—we only have to reconnect with the miracle of life to know this.

Branson's life is all about inspiring goals that challenge the status quo. If there were a common theme to his achievements, it would be that many of his goals have been focused on solving problems and getting past obstacles—similar to a David versus Goliath scenario.

In an interview with Seth Godin, whose recent best seller includes *The Dip and Meatball Sundae*, Richard Branson talks about the common thread that ties the Virgin Empire—from punk rock to space travel—together. [C7:4]

In this interview, Branson describes his approach as being willing to challenge conglomerates (if necessary), offer the best products and the best value, shake up whatever industry you're in, and make sure to have fun doing it. In essence, it's about being bold, going where angels would fear to tread, and enjoying the ride.

But what is forever admirable is his desire to create a business that he'd enjoy doing business with. His ultimate motivation is to serve people. This is why we say that your branding and marketing should not be about your product or services *per se*. It's not about clever, manipulative advertising and promotions. It's about one person essential to all business: *the customer*.

The genius of Branson is his ability to read the pulse of his customers. He is committed to knowing how they think and feel. He understands what they want. He then sets out to provide for those needs and desires in a clear and compelling way that requires little or no explanation.

How well attuned are you with the needs of your customers? Have you taken the time to get to know them and understand them? What problems and obstacles do they have that could become the basis for your next inspiring goal?

Stepping Outside Your Comfort Zone

Taking the high ground will require you to step outside your comfort zone. Branson's approach and direction might appear too risky for some. But remember that avoiding all risk might create an even worse situation for you and your business.

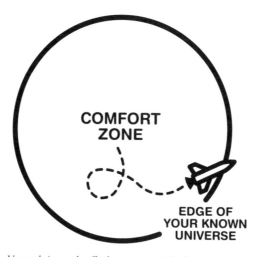

Your audacious goals will take you way outside of your comfort zone.

However, know that we are not advocating that you take mindless risks. Becoming an inspiring entrepreneur has a level of responsibility attached to it. So you need to approach risks with careful thought.

You might be right to say that it's easier for a billionaire than for a small business owner to take risks. Given the lack of financial resources available to small businesses, and the difficulty of battling endless competitors, you will need to be inventive. But the principle of stepping outside your comfort zone is still valid for small businesses. You need to have an inspiring goal for your company to thrive, and that requires you to step outside your comfort zone.

When actor Will Smith said, "Greatness lives on the edge of destruction and the reason someone is great is that they survived death," he was on to something. By stepping outside of your comfort zone you destroy your *limiting* beliefs. By letting go of the constant search for safety you will create the freedom to let your imagination fly.

An Honest Self-Assessment

All great achievements begin with a decision to live life fully and to realize your potential. And it starts with you creating inspiring goals—goals worthy of your time and energy. As we come to the close of this chapter, we encourage you to take some time to be honest with yourself.

We often ask our clients the following question: "Are you inspired by what you do?" The answer is often "yes," but it is suspiciously enthusiastic. Many business owners will swear black and blue about how excited they are about life, but in the next breath they whine and moan about their empty, unfulfilled existence. Sometimes you can see the lack of inspiration in their eyes even though their words paint a different picture.

It is important for you to take stock of where you really are in life. So what do you do when you feel unable to inspire yourself? After all, that is a *huge* task.

As we've said, people like Branson don't deliberately set out to inspire people. They do what they set out to do with all their heart and soul, because they choose to. They identify their why—their purpose, their beliefs, what they love and are passionate about, and in true entrepreneurial fashion, look for ways to combine what they love in the world of business.

Collins and Porras suggest that you consider the following questions to test your BHAG:

- *Does it stimulate forward progress?*
- *Does it create momentum?*
- *Do others find it stimulating, exciting, and adventurous?*
- *Are they willing to throw their creative talents and human energies into it?* C7:5

Imagine how you would feel if you could answer in the affirmative to all these questions. In sharing the story of John Shanahan at *Pyrosales*, John would never claim to be Richard Branson. He is his own person. He has his own Everest to climb. And, his approach is very different to Branson's. However, the entrepreneurial spirit within Branson and others like him is also within John. And it is also within you.

The reason Branson continues to innovate and succeed is that he is so clearly at ease with himself and completely congruent with his brand. Sure, he is a charismatic, cheeky, bright, and a personable showman. But this is not the core of being inspiring.

The important thing is that all inspiring leaders, such as Sir Richard Branson, constantly ask "What if?" questions and look for possibilities. Being realistic does not hold them back and this, in turn, enables them to bring their audacious goals to life.

And *that* is what we find most inspiring.

In the next chapter, we will look at the important role our core values have to play in our lives and work. For you to be inspired by your goals, they must be rooted deeply in your core values. When you consciously connect with your core values, you can then successfully achieve the results you're aiming for.

CHAPTER EIGHT

CORE VALUES: WHAT MATTERS MOST

For a business to thrive, it must have a strong foundation. Just as the tall oak tree has a deep root system that supports and nourishes it, and also prevents it from falling over in a storm, small businesses also need to be firmly grounded. This is certainly true for the Virgin Group.

The Virgin Group consists of more than three hundred branded companies worldwide. It employs approximately fifty thousand people and operates in thirty countries. For most entrepreneurs, the sheer size of this group is unfathomable. People wonder how Richard Branson could not only manage this empire, but also remain enthusiastic and engaged.

Inspiring a team of fifty thousand people, across thirty countries requires more than great leadership and teamwork.

So, how does a company like Virgin remain aligned?

Virgin says: "Our companies are part of a family rather than a hierarchy. They are empowered to run their own affairs, yet the companies help one another, and solutions to problems often come from within the Group somewhere. In a sense we are a commonwealth, with shared ideas, values, interests, and goals." [C8:1]

What is distinct about the Virgin Group is that the root system and foundation of the companies are aligned with Branson's core values—what is important to him. This is definitely the backbone of each of his organizations. It is what supports them and holds them upright.

The Virgin commitment is that "once a Virgin company is up and running, several factors contribute to making it a success." Namely, "the power of the Virgin name and Richard Branson's personal reputation" are among the key criteria. [C8:2]

Core Values: What Are They?

So, what do we mean by *core values?* One of the first books in the genre of management *The Art of Demotivation*, by author E.L. Kersten described core values as *"the values that are most important to the direction of the organization and the decision-making within it."* [C8:3]

Core values, put simply, is your values system—that which you value most. A core value is something you will fight for and defend, and under no circumstances will you consciously compromise it. For some, high value is given to family and friends or financial independence. For others high value is placed on charity, making a difference to the community, human rights, and defending freedom.

Everyone has a set of core values, and not all are the same. In fact, most people are unaware of their core values and often don't understand that every decision we make in life regarding how we spend our money, our time, and our energy will come back to what we *value* most.

While this may sound simple, it isn't. Too often, organizations— large and small—are giving lip service to their core values and aren't aligned with them at all. It is one thing to state them and another to be living by them with absolute conviction.

The Driving Force Within Your Business

When a core value and a decision are constantly out of alignment, inner conflict and turmoil will occur. And we all know the impact in our lives when we aren't living in a way that is congruent with our values. The same is true for a business.

When the core values are neglected, the root system of the company begins to wither and dry up. This then weakens the business because the support system is absent.

That said, we invite you to consider this: Have you sold out on *your* core values? If you have, then consider yourself infected with root rot! It's okay. We've all been here at some point. The important thing to realize is that you've been compromising what is most paramount. We know only too well how negatively impacted an organization can be when personal and business core values are violated.

In *Built to Last: Successful Habits of Visionary Companies*, authors Jim Collins and Jerry Porras say, "Your company must have a set of core values. Each of the visionary companies (that they studied) had established a set of core values in its infancy that still survives today. If it ever came upon hard times, the values would still be retained. They would only be modified in the most extreme cases." [C8:4]

What Collins and Porras are suggesting is that core values are the driving force within a business. They hold the space for members of an organization to remain accountable in working toward a common goal. Without a clear commitment to what it holds to be highly valuable, the business risks not having a clear message or coherent expression in the market.

Your Business is a Reflection of You

So let's look at the criteria Branson has incorporated into every business he has started or bought as a joint venture. These six values are non-negotiable for anything bearing the Virgin label:

- *It must be high quality*
- *It must be innovative*
- *It must provide good value for the money*
- *It must challenge existing alternatives in the market*
- *It must generate a sense of fun*
- *It must deliver brilliant customer service* [C8:5]

If Branson's companies were to compromise any one of these values, then it would no longer be a true reflection of a Virgin company. And you can bet that the Virgin leaders oversee the companies to ensure compliance. Richard Branson realizes that if the core values he holds for his companies are neglected, the brand will depreciate.

If you were to remove the Virgin label and replace it with Richard Branson, you will see that the core values of the business are congruent with who Branson is. They are perfectly aligned. This is because the business is a true reflection of its owner.

On the other hand, if Branson were to change any one of his personal values, this would have a direct influence on the business—perhaps even detrimental consequences.

Throughout all of Branson's companies these six above mentioned values are absolutely non-negotiable. This is what is unique about a values-based organization. The integrity of the foundations is maintained, regardless of the challenges faced.

Leadership and Core Values

The leaders of your enterprise must be aligned with your core values. Leadership begins with a single idea: to accomplish anything, your team must be aligned with your vision and mission. To make this clear, we'll look at another trail-blazing company: The Body Shop.

From its modest beginnings in 1976, The Body Shop has grown to have over two thousand stores in sixty countries, and it is the second largest cosmetic franchise in the world.

Dame Anita Roddick once said of her vision: "I just want The Body Shop to be the best, most breathlessly exciting company—and one that changes the way business is carried out. That is my vision." [C8:6]

As further evidence of how core values are represented within an organization, here is a sample of The Body Shop's mission statement:

- *Dedicate our business to the pursuit of social and environmental change*
- *Creatively balance the financial and human needs of our stakeholders: employees, customers, franchisees, suppliers and shareholders*
- *Courageously ensure that our business is ecologically sustainable, meeting the needs of the present without compromising the future*
- *Meaningfully contribute to local, national, and international communities in which we trade by adopting a code of conduct which ensures care, honesty, fairness and respect*
- *Passionately campaign for the protection of the environment, to defend human rights and against animal testing within the cosmetics industry*
- *Tirelessly work to narrow the gap between principle and practice while making fun, passion, and care part of our daily lives* [C8:7]

These core values are the golden thread that holds together The Body Shop team throughout the world. Each of them works together in a common spirit to ensure that the vision is upheld.

Sadly, Anita Roddick passed away in 2007. Businesswoman, human rights activist, environmental campaigner and best known as the founder of The Body Shop, the legacy that she has left the business community and the world is significant.

Many great business leaders, such as Anita Roddick, know the importance of building their businesses with their core values as the foundation. As the leader of your business, and in order to be a rock star in your field, the lesson is simple: You also must build your business on the foundation of your core values.

Focus On Your Passion

To illustrate how important it is for entrepreneurs to create a business based on their core values, we want to share a case study based on one of Louise's coaching sessions.

This client raised the question about developing a second business and wanted to create a business plan. The reason for sharing this case study is that while it is extremely easy to get excited about an idea and create the business plan, it is a whole different ball game to *live* that business plan while giving due consideration to the importance of your core values.

Too often, entrepreneurs invest time and money in a business plan without even thinking about the greater purpose and values of the company. Equally, if our client was to achieve a different level of success in her new business venture, then something had to change. This goal needed to be based on her core values.

The American poet, actress and leading Civil Rights figure Maya Angelou once said: "Success is liking yourself, liking what you do, and liking how you do it." [C8:8]

With a glint in her eye the client said, "I want to build a

business that turns over tens of millions of dollars with a healthy profit."

No matter what the idea, in the first instance we are committed to encouraging our clients to think big, because you never know what might be motivating the first idea. Therefore, what Louise needed to do was get an understanding of how ready, willing, and able the client was to operate like an owner of a business that would turn over tens of millions of dollars. And had she carefully considered how her core values would serve as the foundation of this business?

Peeling away the layers of the onion is a metaphor for your life. When you take away the day-to-day challenges you will discover the heart, soul, and spirit of your core values.

For the past eight years, this client has owned and operated a healthcare practice. The new business idea was focused on importing a range of healthcare products that could be distributed across Australia to similar practices.

Know Your "Why"

There was no doubt in our minds that the two wouldn't work well together. Like most small business owners, this client had a degree of impatience about getting things moving. However, Louise knew only too well the importance of getting every entrepreneur to articulate their *why*—their reason for choosing their goal and the purpose behind their idea or dream. Because without an understanding of their why, there will be no traction and no real results.

So Louise asked the question: "Why do you want to do this?" The client's response was, "Well, this is the one I've been waiting for." Again Louise asked the question: "So, why do you want to start this business?"

As you can imagine, the client quickly became agitated with Louise repeating the same question. But Louise wasn't moving on until she had extracted a strong enough "why" statement. So, the client's response was, "Louise, this business can give me the money I want. And wouldn't it be exciting to go for a goal like ten million."

Of course she thought she'd done a great job of convincing Louise. However, money is simply a result. So, because Louise didn't want to demoralize her by asking the same question again and again, she reframed the question by asking, "What excites you about this product?"

Well, the client didn't even have to think: "I am passionate about bringing products and services that are chemical and toxin-free, and educating other practitioners about the value of using products like these."

Louise persisted: "What would excite you most about this opportunity? Running a successful business, committed to introducing chemical and toxin-free products or one that turns over ten million dollars?"

For our client, the idea began to crystallize: what she was really passionate about was the difference that this product could make to her customers rather than the money. And by expressing her passion, she was able to realize how important her core values would be in the pursuit of this opportunity.

As entrepreneurs, this is why we need to learn from people like Richard Branson and Anita Roddick. Imagine if you were to invest time and effort in developing a plan purely driven by a profit-focused venture—especially if money is not high on your values list. For our client to experience a different level of success, first she needed to set this business up with the right foundations from day one and align her actions with her core values.

On a personal level, we too have faced our own challenges in the twenty years we have been in business together. However, what we know to be true, is that when you are connected and aligned with what is most important—your core values—you are inspired every day, excited about what you are doing, and view the world through the eyes of possibility.

If on the other hand, you are not aligned with your core values, you become disengaged and disempowered. And quite frankly, if you're not engaged and inspired, what type of clients will you attract?

Your Core Values in An Age of Business Turmoil

Looking at entrepreneurs such as Branson and Roddick, it's easy to see that their personal values are directly tied to the values of their businesses. This tight interconnection between the business owner and their business often generates a legitimate concern among many of our clients.

They worry that this might hinder their ability to sell the business—that the business will be so dependent upon them that there is no way it could survive without them. And there is no question that by developing a personal brand and establishing yourself as a leading authority in your field that there will be a direct link between you and your business.

However, it's important to remember that your core values can live on in the business even if you sell the company and are no longer the owner. The key is to structure your company so your values, like your DNA, can be passed from generation to generation, and to continue to drive your company, long after you are gone. And this is exactly what has transpired within The Body Shop. Understand that a strong personal brand built on lasting values will help your business thrive without you.

What many small business entrepreneurs don't realize is that it's not personal branding that creates a detrimental form of dependency. The real problem is that many business owners often structure their company so it won't operate without them serving as the manager of day-to-day business.

In our book *The Invisible Entrepreneur: How To Grow Your Business by Taking 3 Months Off!,* we clearly outline how entrepreneurs often become the manager of their business by default, thus limiting their ability to be true entrepreneurs. They get trapped in running the show, making it impossible for them to ever take time off work.

If you are one of those entrepreneurs who is the manager by default, then the concept of *The Invisible Branson* may be quite timely for you to re-evaluate your role within your business.

Richard Branson had to structure the Virgin group so that all his companies could run without him being involved in all the details. This freedom has allowed him to be a true entrepreneur, to be involved in marketing his business by education and inspiring his customers and prospects. His business structure allows him to fully live out his personal brand and the core values imbedded in it.

You might still say that if the business is intrinsically linked to you, a buyer would not want to buy it. If that were true, then with the sad passing of Anita Roddick, The Body Shop would have been worthless. Instead, in March 2006, The Body Shop agreed to a £652.3 million takeover by L'Oréal. [C8:9]

How to Catch a Monkey!

The principle here is that you must become the authority in your market, not by accident, but by design.

One more important reason to develop a strong set of core values for you and your company is to help you survive all the changes that will happen in the market over time.

A commitment to a clear set of core values allows you to adapt and adjust to changing situations, but without fear of losing your identity, purpose, mission and long-term objectives. To illustrate this idea, think about the proverbial monkey with the banana.

If you don't know the story, let us tell you how to catch a monkey. You put a banana in a cage. The bars of the cage are just wide enough for the monkey to slip its paw through and grab the banana. The cage is firmly secured by a couple of stakes and left in the jungle where the monkey can find it.

When the monkey discovers the cage with the banana, it gets its paw through the bars and gets hold of the banana. Unfortunately, by gripping the banana the monkey cannot get its paw out. It is stuck with the banana firmly in its grip. This is when the monkey faces its captors. Despite the danger of being captured, the monkey will not let go of the banana.

Businesses Need to Adapt and Change

Sadly, this is what happens to some business owners. They simply hang on to the established, traditional way of running the business—despite knowing that the old methods and strategies are trapping them.

To succeed in today's business world, you need to constantly evaluate what is working and what is not. If you keep doing business the way you did it a few years ago then, like the monkey with the banana, you may bring about your own downfall.

Such restructuring requires a different mindset. Einstein once said: "We cannot solve our problems with the same thinking we used when we created them." C8:10

There is no question that businesses need to adapt and change. But a lasting commitment to a set of overarching and inspiring core values will enable you and your company to maintain a consistent and coherent identity over time. Your personal brand will stand the test of time. Your personal story will go on ahead of you.

When you find the courage to restructure your business and develop a personal brand on the foundation of inspiring core values, you will become free to express yourself fully as a business rock star. And that free expression will enable you to have a great time while making the money you so richly deserve.

Most importantly, when you are *inspired* by the core values of your business, others will be inspired by *you*.

It's an almost universal truth that the most inspiring companies are those built on the value of making a positive impact in the community and the world. In other words, one of the primary core values for every business—as Branson has shown us—is to make the world a better place. It's to this subject that we turn next.

CHAPTER NINE

MAKING A DIFFERENCE

It's Tuesday September 1, 2002 at around 10 a.m. We are in Lake Como, Italy. We are on our first three-month holiday. This was the holiday that became the basis for our book *The Invisible Entrepreneur: How to Grow Your Business by Taking 3 Months Off!*

Sitting on the balcony, we finished our breakfast and were enjoying the tranquility of the beautiful lake. There were mountains on either side and a whitish grey church with a bell tower gracefully nestled in the midst of the peaks. The scenery was simply breathtaking.

We were watching boats of all shapes and sizes skim around the lake, making their way to various destinations at a leisurely pace—then disappearing from our view. The large boats were leaving a wake that seemed to last forever. But the small dinghies hardly disturbed the stillness of the water.

As we watched this beautiful scene, I (William) couldn't help thinking that the wakes made by the large ships were similar to the legacy we leave behind when we make a difference in the lives of others. Some people—those who work hard to help others—are remembered for an eternity. Others—like the dinghies—say goodbye and are gone in the blink of an eye, having hardly made a wave.

And I wondered: Can small business entrepreneurs leave a powerful and lasting legacy?

Leave a Lasting Legacy

The answer is *yes*. Richard Branson is similar to one of those large boats on Lake Como, a leader who leaves a huge wake. His presence has already impacted every part of the globe. The legacy of this man will live on for centuries to come. Because of him, we will never do business the same way again.

That might sound like a big claim.

After all, he wasn't the first business leader to introduce low airfares. Sir Freddie Laker was really the man who blazed the trail for Branson to follow. And it's not that Branson is the richest man on the planet. There are many people who are richer than he is. There are also many business leaders who, like him, are smart, courageous and innovative.

The reason Branson leaves such a generous legacy is because he demonstrates that you can run a successful business and stay strongly focused on seeking the greater good.

In a global market, this is not typically the way most enterprise leaders want to do business. On the contrary, most multi-national corporations think almost exclusively about the stakeholders, not the customers or the community at large.

In business today, the reality is that we will be lied to, manipulated, and exploited for the sake of profits. This is how the game is played.

Yet, no matter what may happen in the future, Branson has shown that a business can make money while contributing to the greater good.

It's an important distinction, and worth further thought. This way of thinking was eloquently communicated by the late John F. Kennedy at his inaugural ceremony when he said: "Ask not what your country can do for you. Ask what you can do for your country." In other words, Kennedy made a call for people to contribute—not just take, take, take. [C9:1]

Doing Business With Your Head and Your Heart

Among Branson's core values, one of the most important is his constant goal of finding ways to contribute to the greater good. This way of doing business—to benefit the community at large and not just the stakeholders' bottom line—can also be explained through Hindu or Buddhist philosophy. We would describe Branson as a person with an open-heart chakra.

Chakra is a concept originating from Hindu and Buddhist practice. There are seven chakras, or energy centers, located along the spine at the major branches of the nervous system. The chakras begin at the base of the spinal column and move up toward to the top of the skull. To learn more about chakras we highly recommend searching on Google. For now, the heart chakra is the fourth of the seven; it determines your ability to express love to yourself and others.

Doing business with your heart is still not something endorsed in the West. In fact, until recently this has been actively discouraged. However, times are changing. We can no longer operate from the basis of, "It is a dog-eat-dog world, and we must look after our own self-interests at all costs." This way of operating is diametrical to the concept of "for the greater good."

While we'll never know, it's worth considering whether or not the global financial crisis would have occurred if all those who were responsible had operated with a consciousness of the greater good of all.

The same can be asked of a small business owner. Your customers expect you to provide value for money. They also expect the companies who sell them products and services to act in an ethical, responsible way. As the head of your organization, it is crucial for you to honor that trust by going the extra mile.

This is not a fad or a "nice thing to do." When money is tight, it is easy to put the needs of the broader community on the back burner and say, "We'll do more for the community some day when we have enough profits." Or, "Helping others is great for people like Branson who have the money, but I'm just a simple person with few resources."

Frankly, there is no reason why a small business can't make some kind of contribution to the broader community. If we do not look after our community and the planet, future generations will wind up in dire straits. And doing the right thing for the community does not mean that a company has to forfeit commercial advantages. Profit and community contributions don't need to be mutually exclusive.

Everything is Connected

Our planet is going through massive changes. You only have to read the newspaper or listen to the news and you'll quickly see that our understanding of the Earth and our relationship to it has never mattered more.

In the 1970s, James Lovelock and Lynn Margulis put forward a supposition called The Gaian Paradigm, which states that the

Earth is a living system. The theory asserts that living organisms and their inorganic surroundings have evolved together as a single living system that greatly affects the chemistry and conditions of Earth's surface. *C9:2*

Some scientists believe that this "Gaian system" self-regulates global temperature, atmospheric content, ocean salinity, and other factors in an "automatic" manner.

Earth's living system appears to keep conditions on our planet just right for life to exist! Therefore, it is our responsibility to preserve our planet for future generations, to collectively do what we can for the good of those who come after us.

You can see more and more corporate leaders like Branson working from this global perspective. Likewise, you and your small business can make a contribution—no matter how small your company might be. Acting for the greater good does not have to be at the expense of your business. The goodwill you generate adds value to your brand. It can also be a catalyst for generating more sales. So it is a win/win situation.

No matter how big or small your business is you can make a difference. Branson's focus is about making the greatest difference to the greatest number of people.

The Purpose of Your Business

What we mean by the "greater good" is this: the greatest good for the greatest number of people. As you can see in the last diagram, you are the center of your reality. You can choose to be self-centered, and focus only on goals that make a difference to you. Or, you can align your goals and your business in a way that has the greatest benefit to all.

Since the global financial crisis, there is an underlying tension, an uncertainty in the marketplace. Money is tight. Business owners are a lot more cautious in taking even the most basic calculated risks. Therefore, the question is: How can an owner of a small business operate for the greater good? And, while it would be normal to take care of *numero uno,* it is much more sustainable for our world if we all played the game for the greater good.

Branson has spoken openly about the dirty trick campaigns by other airlines. But to operate the Branson way, you need to go back to a very basic level and ask this simple question: What is the purpose of my business?

At one point, I (William) measured my success by the amount of money I earned. In the pursuit of money, I became an emotional cripple. Money doesn't provide happiness. If it did, all the rich people would be unbelievably happy. Yet, they aren't any different, nor are they any better than you or I.

Money certainly provides freedom to obtain what your heart desires. What Branson has exemplified is how you can have both.

Greater Good is Great for Marketing

Marketing activities must be focused on the one person who is essential to all business: the customer. If your customers know that the way you do business not only benefits them, but also the wider community, how would they feel? Wouldn't they want to do more business with you?

This is not about giving lip service to customers and community service. Branson's model of running profitable businesses, while also serving the community, has turned the world upside down.

We are told that global aviation currently accounts for more than two percent of global carbon dioxide emissions. In time this will increase. Richard Branson's Virgin Atlantic is spearheading the search for alternative fuels. Qatar Airways, Continental Airlines, and British Airways, among others, are following the lead of Virgin Atlantic to test various biofuel blends.

You can bet Virgin Atlantic will gain a lot of positive PR because of their efforts to protect the environment. Yet most entrepreneurs believe that doing the right thing is an expense because they don't understand how to capitalize on the good they do.

Branson has proven you can build a brand and a business on the strength of doing the right thing for the customer. That makes it easier to understand how you can do the same. You don't have to reinvent the wheel.

Ordinary People Being Extraordinary

The following stories demonstrate that you don't have to run a big business to take the high ground. As we have said, we work with many talented and dedicated entrepreneurs who epitomize that ordinary people can achieve extraordinary outcomes. Here are three entrepreneurs who have become business rock stars. Our first story is about Margaret Brockie.

Story of Margaret Brockie

Margaret Brockie was a nutrition teacher. After her husband passed away, she wanted to do something—take on a new challenge, make a difference, and leave a lasting legacy. Her mantra was "I am not ready to retire."

What is unique about Margaret is that on her sixtieth birthday she decided to manufacture and market her own brand of the most nutritional breakfast cereal on the planet: Brockie's Breakfast Cereal. And over the last fifteen years or so Margaret has been able to make a massive difference in her community. Most people believe that at her age she should have been ready to retire.

The fact that she had no experience in marketing and that she was under capitalized didn't faze her. What she had was an abundance of passion and enthusiasm. And she capitalized on these qualities to the max. The most extraordinary help and support flowed in and does so to this day.

What drove Margaret was her passion to teach people about healthy eating. And she wanted to share the importance of good food and its rewards. She didn't try to be a super sales person, or an extraordinary marketer. Instead, she became a teacher.

Her forte was the stage, talking to large groups. To get keynote engagements she constantly put herself at risk by approaching event organizers. She fearlessly called radio and TV stations, editors and journalists. She always accepted the opportunity to talk at events.

Every media and speaking success translated into having Brockie's Brekky in more delicatessens, health food shops, cafés, restaurants, supermarkets, and even on the menus of Government House and Parliament House.

Margaret has been an inspiration to us and many others who have had the privilege of working closely with her. And what an extraordinary difference she has made over the past fifteen years.

The next chapter to this story is that Margaret has sold her business. Having been recently diagnosed with cancer, her time and energy is now being diverted to her own health and lifestyle. Her mantra has now become "I am not ready to die." Thankfully her extraordinary spirit is alive and well and she is following her passion for making the best of her own health now by destressing her life and co-operating with the help of the National Institute of Integrative Medicine to fully recover.

Margaret used to say, "I want to change the way Australians eat," so she is thrilled that a dedicated couple have chosen to continue producing Brockie's Breakfast Cereal. After all, we all have to eat right!

Story of Rosalyn Manipis

Our second story is about a young mom. Although half the age of Margaret—she is a powerful and dynamic woman in her own right.

Rosalyn has three children—a massive job on it's own. Having come from a Filipino background, Rosalyn has witnessed first hand the heartache of underprivileged children who don't have access to toys. This is the passion that drove her to give up her full time job as a nurse to launch her own online toy business, as well as a charity with the goal of collecting toys for underprivileged children in both Australia and overseas.

Rosalyn could easily have given up on this desire to make a difference to children. She had good reason, having a young family of her own. On the other hand, Rosalyn has discovered that while operating her online toy store and toy charity, opportunities have shown up, doors have opened, and her network has dramatically expanded.

Story of Bernie Mitchell

Our third story is about Bernie Mitchell, a business leader and author of a book about bipolar disorder.

Bernie is the successful owner of a residential property management business in Sydney, Australia. For many years, he harbored a terrible secret, or so he thought. His secret? He suffered from bipolar disorder. Bernie says this: "Can you imagine that I have to hide the fact from the vast majority of people I meet for fear of setting off their prejudices against mental health challenges?"

Bernie has not only taken the initiative to overcome his bipolar disorder but is also deeply saddened by the heartlessness of many people who have stigmatized those who suffer from this disorder. He now has had the courage to demystify bipolar disorder in the business world by writing a book about his journey. While you might think that writing a book will make him money, this is Bernie's way of giving back to the community.

Your Business is a Living, Breathing Organism

Just as James Lovelock and Lynn Margulis proposed that the Earth is a living system, we put forth the proposition that your business is a living, breathing organism with a heart and a spirit.

Because your business is a reflection of who you are, what would happen if you were to live in fear that the future for you is uncertain, that there is a lack of resources, that money is tight, and that business is tough? Consider the negative ripple effect that this would have on not only your business and the people you work with, but the community at large!

By comparison, when you do business with Virgin, Google, or Apple, how do you feel? There is something different and dynamic about these businesses. Even when there is no one around, you can feel the difference.

There is no reason why owners of small businesses can't be inspired by the way Richard Branson does business. Through his business, he has made a remarkable and positive contribution to the world. So, why not you? You are no different than Branson.

The point is this: Achieving extraordinary success would be a contribution to you, your family, your team, and your community. As a result, the planet itself will benefit. There are so many other individuals and businesses who depend on your success.

They say that when a butterfly flaps its wings it could lead to the creation of a hurricane. In the same way, when you serve the greater good, you never know what ripple effect you might make.

Will there be obstacles? Will there be hurdles to jump, problems to solve, and difficulties to overcome? Certainly! But as we will show in our next chapter, most of our problems stem from not fully understanding how to overcome our problems. Read on and we'll help you face the challenging realities of life in a life-changing way.

But before you turn the page, we want to share one more story. A good friend of ours—and also one of our consultants, died very suddenly at a relatively young age. Shelly Freeman was born in Cincinnati, Ohio and later made her home in Sydney, Australia.

At her funeral there was a little booklet about Shelly for everyone to take home. Among many photos of Shelly in the booklet, there was this poem by Linda Ellis. It read:

> *"For it matters not how much we own, the cars . . . the house . . . the cash. What matters is how we live and love and how we spend our dash."* [C9:3]

CHAPTER TEN

INTEGRITY: THE FOUNDATION FOR SUCCESS

Imagine what would happen to the Virgin brand and Richard Branson's credibility if every week the media headlines screamed: "Branson Reneges!" Or "Another Broken Branson Promise," or "Branson Backflips on Space Venture!" You would put him in the category of some untrustworthy politician rather than the innovative businessman he actually is.

And, if Richard Branson broke his word and did not deliver on his promises, many journalists would have a field day. His reputation would be in tatters. The damage to his brand would be *irreversible*.

The same is true for your business. You are its core; your business is a reflection of you. If you gain a reputation for not keeping your word, your business will suffer accordingly. And the purpose for looking at this aspect is that the more you are in the spotlight, the harder it is to slip under the radar. As you develop your personal brand and become a business rock star, it's crucial to understand that any blemish to your reputation will show up like a drop of coffee on a pristine white shirt.

Now in cases such as rock bands, celebrities, athletes, and politicians, we've seen that bad press and controversy actually strengthens their reputation and creates a following. In fact, some people will go so far as hero-worship the bad behavior. You only have to recall in more recent times the publicity generated about people such as Tiger Woods, Hugh Grant, Shane Warne, and Paris Hilton.

However, in this chapter we want to discuss the word integrity and what this really means in the world of entrepreneurship.

What is Integrity?

Integrity is simply doing what you say you are going to do. When your actions cease to be aligned with your words, you are out of integrity. This is what makes Richard Branson unique. Don't worry, we are not under any illusion that he is a saint, nor are we inferring that he is perfect on every level. However, he never fails to deliver on his promises.

Regarding integrity, please understand that this is not about you becoming a goody two-shoes. Nor has it anything to do with you becoming some kind of saint or needing to get everything perfect. And although there are many people who we deem to be saints and extraordinary human beings, such as Nelson Mandela, Dr. Martin Luther King Jr., and Mother Teresa, this is about living your life based on your commitment to integrity.

Our definition of integrity also has nothing to do with morality. Morality is defined by group consensus. The Oxford

Dictionary defines morality as the "principles concerning the distinction between right and wrong or good and bad behavior." [C10:1] This is not what we mean by integrity. Our focus is about you keeping your promises.

We realize that in the commercial environment, there are varying degrees of interpretation regarding the word integrity. Therefore, the highest form of keeping your word is when you are at one with it and you operate like your word matters.

We'll say it again—we're not suggesting that you have to be some kind of saint—but you need to follow through on what you say you'll do. You must meet the standards you espouse or even exceed them rather than let your customers down or the people who matter in your life. As a customer you would expect this, and this is what your customers will expect from you.

Consequences of Breaking Your Word

Business owners pay a hefty penalty when they fail to keep their word. Whether it's admitted in public or not, people tend to suffer from feelings of guilt, shame, and embarrassment as a consequence of failing to keep their word. They might say, "I want to crawl into a hole and disappear." They might cross the road to avoid people they have let down. Or they start behaving in ways that deflect the responsibility, such as with anger or by blaming external circumstances.

However, the impact of consistently breaking your word is that you lose your power. Your self-esteem takes a beating. As a result, you lose energy and will no longer be as effective as you know you're capable of being. Left unchecked, this will have a profound effect on your business and your bottom line.

Every human being has experienced this in one form or another. And, it occurs when you compromise on your core values. It usually happens when you say "yes" and agree to do something that you really have no intention of being committed to. And it irks you that you've sold yourself short.

On the outside you may still be perceived as a success, but on the inside you know it is all a disguise and that someday it will all catch up with you.

Therefore, if Branson were to renege on his promises, there is no way that you'd trust him. And, you would sense a lack of authenticity about his charming, cheery, and irreverent personality.

We speculate that at the heart of Branson's power, vitality, and passion is his integrity. Branson's heart pumps integrity into the vital organs of his companies, and that in turn is manifested visibly in his success.

Branson walks his talk. This quality is contagious. Without this attribute he would be just another figurehead of a multinational corporation willing to exploit everyday people, those who are his customers.

This is not to suggest that Branson doesn't want his business to also be about making a profit. In business this is the underlying point; however, isn't it great to know that you can make a profit and not compromise on your values?

Integrity in the Reality of Commerce

In the fast-paced commercial environment, it's tough to keep your word. And while it is a commonly accepted norm to talk about best practices, it is rare to see these best practices actually in operation.

One need only look to the old truism that every company tells their customers: "You are a valued client, an appreciated customer; you are more than just a number."

However, customers know that this is not true 100 percent of the time and that ultimately the company has no intention of treating them as valued customers.

More importantly, if an organization's communications and actions are not aligned, then customers do not feel valued. Such bad habits are nonetheless tolerated. Too often consumers just put up with it.

Take for instance that we can put up with drug companies lying about the side effects of medications. Unless it is of high enough importance, we eat genetically modified food without even knowing it. Vegetables that are supposed to be fresh have been in a deep freezer for months on end. There are hidden bank charges you did not know about and you have been paying them for years.

Welcome to reality. This is the world we put up with. Or do we?

There was a time when everyone believed that the earth was flat. If you said otherwise, people would think you were mad. Today, if you were to speculate that the earth is flat you would be laughed at.

Somewhere along the way there was a shift in thinking and we discovered the earth was, in fact, round. In much the same way, this is what Branson has done in ensuring that the commercial decisions at Virgin are made *with* the customer in mind.

Integrity in Leadership

The bottom line is that integrity is a matter of leadership. Your business is a reflection of you in the same way that the Virgin group is a reflection of Richard Branson. He has proven that a great business does not equate with greed, and that you do not have to exclusively look after your own interests and ignore everyone else.

Using the analogy of a bicycle wheel, the leader of a business is its hub, and the hub is the center. The conventional bicycle wheel, for single-rider bikes, commonly has between 28 to 36 spokes and can carry around seven hundred times its own weight before it succumbs to gravity.

Think of the spokes as being your team members, and the wheel as the point where your business interfaces with your customers—where the rubber meets the road. If you were to take out each spoke one by one, at some point the wheel will collapse due to the lack of support.

The bicycle wheel is a metaphor for your business: When it loses its integrity,
there's a point at which your business becomes unworkable.

Could this happen with your business? Absolutely. And while you can have every intention to treat your customers well and deliver on the promises you make, if any of your team members fails to deliver, it will jeopardize your good name. If enough people on the team are running their own agendas, then the whole company is at risk.

Take Formula One racing, for example. Just imagine if one of the support crew from the Ferrari team decided he wouldn't give his best during the pit stop. Or what would happen if the Socceroos' goalkeeper decided to not give his best? Or what if the Australian Davis Cup team just went through the motions?

As you can see, one person can affect the entire team. Therefore, it's critical to understand that you are the captain of the team and everyone takes his or her lead from you.

Now you might claim that as a small business operator you can't possibly manage every facet of what happens with your team. Well, consider that Branson has managed to infuse his company's *ethos* across the entire Virgin group. Therefore, one way or another, your leadership—for better or worse—will affect your entire company; so it's better to make sure that you're leading with integrity.

Branson became the benchmark for his company—someone to emulate. Whatever he stood for had to be delivered by his team, *no matter what*. When you board a Virgin flight, there's an expectation that you will be served by Sir Richard Branson—and he does—through the crew he has recruited.

On a recent trip back from the United States, we were delayed at the Los Angeles airport and had the good fortune to connect with one of the Virgin crew. Rather than tell us that they worked for an airline, they claimed to work for Sir Richard. Now that is what we call respect, and it is more than possible for any business owner to garner this in their business.

Integrity and Your Team

When building a personal brand, what *you* do certainly counts. However, this principle also extends to your team. If you are to make a strong personal brand a reality, you need the right people doing the right things.

Jim Collins, in his best seller *Good to Great*, asks you to imagine your company is a bus and you are the driver. It is at a standstill and it's your job to get it going. Collins says, "When it comes to getting started, good-to-great leaders understand three simple truths.

First, if you begin with 'who,' you can more easily adapt to a fast-changing world." The second truth is: "If you have the right people on your bus, you don't need to worry about motivating them. The right people are self-motivated."

And finally, the third truth is this: "You may be headed in the right direction, but you still won't achieve greatness. Great vision with mediocre people still produces mediocre results." *C10:2*

Branson equally knows that having the right people is essential to progress. No matter which *Virgin* flight you're on, you are left with a strong *Virginesque* feeling that lingers with you long after the flight. This brand personality *is* Richard Branson. It gets delivered no matter who the flight crew are. It may be Branson or Joe Bloggs, but the service will be very much the same.

So what about the people around you? Do you think they will deliver on the promises *you* make? If not, the total organization will be impacted. Despite this threat, the golden rule of business is that no matter how bad things get, you have to keep the doors of possibility and opportunity open.

In our book *The Invisible Partnership,* we discussed the power of creating a Mark II version of your business. Mark II means that you get to design a new ideal version of the business exactly as you envision it operating. Then, with this new design, you begin to see the gaps between your existing business and the ideal. In redesigning your company to be like the ideal, the starting point is to make sure you have the right people in place.

When You Break Your Word

No matter how good your intentions are, at some point you will break your word. You cannot avoid this. However, when you do, at least own up to it. There is nothing worse than pretending nothing has happened—like the elephant in the living room scenario. And when you do come clean, then recommit to doing as you say.

We have all read about the movie stars and business leaders

living in the limelight who get caught on the wrong side of the law. While some go through a hopeless act of contesting that they are innocent, others step up and take responsibility.

For instance when Martha Stewart landed herself in hot water with the law, she realized she had to accept responsibility and own up to her errors rather than drag out the process by blaming others or justifying herself. Martha stated that the decision was hard, but necessary. She knew she had to get on with her life and her business. Instead of wallowing in misery, she owned up and recommitted to what was important to her.

The same happened with Hugh Grant on the Jay Leno show. After being caught for picking up a prostitute on the streets of Hollywood, Grant went on national TV to say he was sorry. Tiger Woods approached his problems in a similar way.

Therefore, if you make a mistake, the most effective solution is to come clean. Branson has never tried to make excuses for his failed business ventures. He has, however, been committed to learning from them.

Integrity in Action

When I (William) first gained an understanding of the concept of integrity, I grappled with it. I took it to mean that I must watch everything I said and did. It seemed like one more burden and responsibility; and at the time I already had too many of those.

Writer Lawrence Pearsall Jacks, in his book *Education Through Recreation*, wrote: "A master in the art of living draws no sharp distinction between his work and his play, his labor and his leisure, his mind and his body, his education and his recreation." [C10:3]

Jacks is saying that the key to living a life of integrity, without it being a burden, is to live in a holistic, unified way. While it might seem as though Branson is involved in a lot of different, and random activities, he is living life in a holistic manner.

Jacks goes on to note that a person who lives this way "hardly knows which is which. He simply pursues his vision of excellence through whatever he is doing and leaves others to determine whether he is working or playing. To himself, he always seems to be doing both. Enough for him that he does it well."

When a person comes together in heart, mind, and spirit, their actions are aligned with their words—regardless of whether they are in a business environment, engaging in a promotional event, or just having fun.

Life becomes so much simpler when there is no demarcation between work and play. "I don't think of work as work and play as play," says Branson. "It's all living." [C10:4]

There is much we can learn from Branson. And the reason why we don't see any negative publicity about Branson is that he does what he says he will do. It's as simple as that.

A major aspect of integrity is to live in a way that is consistent with your true identity. In other words, you can't claim to be a person of integrity and then create a false image of yourself. It is vitally important to understand yourself deeply. This self-knowledge, as we will show in the next chapter, is the true foundation for your personal brand.

CHAPTER ELEVEN

ARCHETYPES:
YOU AND YOUR BUSINESS

A personal brand is not about creating a false image of yourself; it's about making your true identity the personal face of your company and expanding on your professional experience to become a recognized leader in your field. In the case of Branson, what you see is what you get.

From our perspective, Branson is not only congruent with who he is but also in what he sets out to achieve. And this is why we have chosen to focus on the subject of archetypes, and the role they play in your life as well as in your business, in this chapter. But more importantly we will be looking at *you* as an archetypal being.

Let's be clear. Archetypes are not some new age term. They have been present in folklore and literature for thousands of years, and they can even be found in prehistoric artwork. The origin of the archetype hypothesis dates back to the time of Plato. *C11:1*

Archetypes have also heavily influenced film screenwriters and directors. For example you only have to consider films such as the *Star Wars* trilogy, *The Lion King*, and the many series of *The Matrix*, *Batman*, *Indiana Jones* and *Harry Potter*, to find evidence of this.

What is an Archetype?

The purpose of discussing this topic with you is that archetypes are equally at play in our lives as well as in our businesses, albeit not consciously visible or known. They play a significant role in allowing us to understand, and gain a deeper level of insight into our core identities, and how we can begin to translate this into our personal brands.

The term archetype is based on the work advanced by Carl Gustav Jung, who was a Swiss psychiatrist and often considered the first modern psychologist. He was an influential thinker along with being the founder of Analytical Psychology. *C11:2*

Jung argued that archetypes are the models upon which we pattern ourselves: they are symbols recognized by all. He believed that there are universal character types that he named archetypes.

In the context of marketing and branding, twelve key archetypes have been identified which symbolize a basic human need, an aspiration or a motivation. Each archetype has its own set of values, meanings and personality traits. *C11:3*

Below is a very brief overview of each archetype, as identified by Jung and then built on by many others. As this is a fascinating topic, we highly recommend that you delve deeper in this subject, and explore it fully. For now when you read this list see which archetype most resonates with you.

The 12 Archetypes C11:4

The Innocent: a person characterized by being wholesome, pure, forgiving, trusting, honest, happy, optimistic, open, and someone who enjoys simple pleasures.

The Explorer: a searcher and seeker, someone adventurous, restless, independent, self-directed, self-sufficient, and who values excitement and freedom.

The Sage: a thinker, philosopher, reflective expert, adviser, teacher; a person who is confident, in control, self-contained, and credible.

The Regular Guy/Girl: an unpretentious straight-shooter who is people-oriented, reliable, dependable, practical, down-to-earth; a person who values routines, predictability, the status quo, and tradition.

The Lover: a person who seeks true love, passion, intimacy, and sensuality. He or she is passionate, sexy, seductive, erotic, and constantly seeks the pleasure to indulge in and follow their emotions.

The Jester: a person who is a clown and trickster, a playful one who takes things lightly, creates a little fun and chaos and lives in the moment in an impulsive, spontaneous way.

The Hero: a competitive and aggressive warrior who is principled. An idealist who challenges wrongs, improves the world and makes proud, courageous, and brave sacrifices for the greater good.

The Outlaw: a person who is rebellious, shocking, outrageous, disruptive, feared, powerful, counter-cultural, revolutionary, and liberated.

The Magician: a shaman and healer. A person who is spiritual, holistic, charismatic, intuitive, and who values magical moments and special rituals; a catalyst for change.

The Caregiver: an altruistic, selfless, nurturing, compassionate, sympathetic, supportive, and generous person.

The Creator: innovative, imaginative, artistic, experimental, willing to take risks, ambitious, and with a strong desire to turn ideas into reality.

The Ruler: a manager and organizer who has a "take charge" attitude; efficient, productive, confident, responsible, and a role model.

Your Primary Archetype

If this is the first time you're hearing about archetypes, you're likely to have connected with two or three of these descriptions. However, upon further reflection there will be one archetype that will start to stand out for you.

Your primary archetype will resonate with you the most because it will provide you with an insight into *why* you do what you do—in life as well as in business. It's not uncommon to see how the entrepreneur's personal archetype is expressed, or acted out, in their business. For instance, let's speculate what the primary archetype is for Richard Branson.

We see a strong connection with the "Hero" as his primary archetype: An idealist who challenges wrongs, improves the world and makes proud, courageous, and brave sacrifices for the greater good. Over the years, we've seen many of his "David versus Goliath" battles.

We equally see aspects of the "Outlaw" influence as his secondary archetype: A person who is rebellious, shocking, outrageous, disruptive, feared, powerful, counter-cultural, revolutionary, and liberated.

As you will see, the nature of how the archetypes are played out in organizations can be quite fascinating.

Archetypes and Your Core Values

A key question we are often asked is: How do the archetypes fit in with your core values? As described in Chapter Eight, your core values are something you will fight for, and defend. They are your values system. How you express your core values, in business and in life, is through your primary archetype.

For instance, if you place high value on wanting to make a difference in the world, but are the type of person who takes on challenges that even angels fear to tip toe into, then you would be described as the Hero archetype. You'll probably find yourself saying: *"Where there's a will, there's a way."*

In contrast, if you were committed to making a difference by helping others, then you'll probably hear yourself saying, *"Love your neighbor as yourself."* And, you would be described as the Caregiver archetype.

Being able to understand your archetype will assist you to align the way you do business, just as Branson has done. This alignment and congruency will save you a great deal of time and money in the long-term.

Archetypes and Marketing

No doubt you've heard terms like positioning, brand personality, or brand character. It's the course number 101 of marketing to create a personality that will differentiate you from your competitors.

As we've seen with the Virgin brand, archetypes have a number of important implications for an organization that go far beyond simple marketing communications. Archetypal images represent fundamental human desires that evoke deep emotions.

These images apply to brands just as much as they do to people; that's exactly why they are so helpful in assisting you to develop your personal brand. In the world of marketing, this is called creating a coherent branding strategy that helps align all modes of communication.

Too often, small businesses don't focus on a branding strategy because the owners aren't spending money on advertising or promotions. They're focused on generating sales rather than on building a brand. But having a brand strategy, will aid small business owners. And understanding how your primary archetype is played out in the business environment will have enormous benefits.

Organizations and Archetypes

Each archetype has a very distinct nature, as well as a key motto and a goal that is associated with it. As you read the following information,[C11:5] we highly recommend that you start to consider how your marketing and promotional message can be aligned with your primary archetype.

The Innocent

Their motto is *"Free to be you and me"* and the goal is to be happy. The strategy is to do things right. An example of organizations associated with this archetype are: Disney World, Dove, and Coca-Cola.

The Explorer

Their motto is *"Don't fence me in"* and the goal is to experience a better, more authentic and more fulfilling life. The strategy is focused on seeking out and experiencing new things. Organizations associated with this archetype are: Jeep, Trope-Snacks, Marlboro, Bounty, and some of the Virgin products.

The Sage

Their motto is *"The truth will set you free."* The goal is to use intelligence and analysis to understand the world. This strategy is focused on seeking out information and knowledge, self-reflection, and understanding thought processes. Organizations associated with this archetype are: Oprah, CNN, Gallup, McKinsey & Co, and Google.

The Regular Guy / Girl

Their motto is *"All men and women are created equal"* and the goal is to belong. The strategy is to develop ordinary solid virtues—be down to earth. Organizations associated with this archetype are: IKEA and Visa.

The Lover

Their motto is *"You're the only one."* The goal is about being in a relationship with the people they love and in surroundings they love. The strategy is to become more and more physically and emotionally attractive. Organizations associated with this archetype are: Alfa Romeo and Haagen-Dazs.

The Jester

Their motto is *"You only live once."* The goal is to have a great time and lighten up the world. The strategy is to play, make jokes, and be funny. Organizations associated with this archetype are: Xbox and Pepsi.

The Hero

Their motto is *"Where there's a will, there's a way."* The goal is focused on improving the world. The strategy is to be as strong and competent as possible. Organizations associated with this archetype are: Nike, Tag Heuer, Duracell, and Virgin.

The Outlaw

Their motto is *"Rules are made to be broken."* The goal is to overturn what isn't working. The strategy is to disrupt, destroy, or shock. Organizations associated with this archetype are: Harley-Davidson, Diesel, and Virgin Airlines.

The Magician

Their motto is *"I make things happen."* The goal is to make dreams come true. The strategy is to develop a vision and live by it. Organizations associated with this archetype are: Apple, Axe, Smirnoff, and Polaroid.

The Caregiver

Their motto is *"Love your neighbour as yourself."* The goal is to help others. The strategy is doing things for others. Organizations associated with this archetype are: Heinz, Volvo and Amnesty International.

The Creator

Their motto is *"If you can imagine it, it can be done."* The goal is to realize a vision. The strategy is to develop artistic control and skill. Organizations associated with this archetype are: Lego, Sony, and Swatch.

The Ruler

Their motto is *"Power isn't everything, it's the only thing."* The goal is to create a prosperous successful family or community. The strategy is to exercise power. Organizations associated with this archetype are: IBM and Mercedes-Benz.

There is no doubt that being able to personally identify with your primary archetype is a powerful process. However, as an entrepreneur, having your business be consciously aligned with your primary archetype will provide clarity for you, your team, and your customers. It will also ensure that there is a consistent message being promoted at all times.

For example, if you think Volvo, you'll think safety. Safety aligns perfectly with the Caregiver archetype. The goal of this archetype is to help others. For as long as we can remember, Volvo's single message has been focused on safety.

Now let's look at Domino's Pizza and how their archetype became their point of difference. The reason for choosing Domino's Pizza is to highlight that you can successfully create a marketing campaign without relying on an individual or a "face" for the brand.

Your Point of Difference

Domino's Pizza makes pizzas from the same ingredients as everyone else and yet holds a significant market share. They have achieved this by creating the brand personality of the "Hero" archetype. And what does a hero do?

In the case of Domino's Pizza, the hero will deliver your pizza within just thirty minutes of ordering. Like the knight in shining armor, Domino's comes to the rescue of the hungry customers.

This is a characteristic that their target demographic associates with the brand. It is all about conveying the emotional associations—not the rational. The whole point of brand personality is to add a differentiating dimension to a brand that the product alone cannot convey—because in reality all pizzas are much the same.

Back in 1973, Domino's Pizza rolled out a creative new ad campaign that guaranteed that their customers would get their pizza within thirty minutes of placing their orders. This was a very innovative idea at the time: "If it's not there in thirty minutes, it's free."

Is that to say that other pizza stores don't offer the same service? No, they do. However, there is an old saying in marketing which goes: "He who first speaks the truth, preempts the truth."

The promise to deliver on time often got Domino's into trouble and they had to abandon it in 1993 after a St. Louis woman who was involved in a car accident with a Domino's delivery person sued the company on the grounds that the thirty-minute pledge led to accidents. [C11:6]

Obviously Domino's went to extreme lengths to deliver on their promises. However, this is something that even a modest business could do to create a point of difference by creating a brand personality according to the principles of the Jungian archetypes. But first you need to do something that ninety percent of businesses either neglect or fail to do properly.

Know Your Customers

Think about it. In order to fulfill your customer's needs, you need to take the time to understand what they are. There's no real surprise that companies who do understand their customers' needs end up with the majority of the market share.

Let's go back to what Domino's did. They found out by connecting with their customers that the most important factor was getting their pizzas delivered in the shortest possible time.

This is where the knight in shining armor came to the rescue. One hour is just too long for a hungry belly, so they emphasized delivery in thirty minutes. This is the power that focusing on customer needs can have in helping create a brand personality.

However, how you go about providing brilliant customer service will be very unique to you. The same is true for how Virgin delivers their customer service compared with say Qantas or Singapore Airlines. We all have our own way of doing business.

In small business how you do what you do is inherently who you are. Rather than attempting to adopt some other way, you know what suits you best. Now imagine you are the head of Domino's. Review the previous lists of archetypes and identify what your motto would be and how you would go about delivering a pizza within thirty minutes of receiving the order.

Identifying Your Archetype

While it's not uncommon for a corporation to create an archetype based entirely on what the customer wants, this is not what we are suggesting that you should do. When it comes to creating a brand for a person, the brand personality must not only focus on the customer's needs but must also be in keeping with your true self. And this is what Richard Branson has always done.

In the case of your personal brand, you need to look at what is in keeping with your core values and archetype, not just the market. This is especially applicable to small businesses because the business is a reflection of the owner. It must be congruent with who you are.

This congruence will be reflected back to your customers. And, they are more likely to do business with you if there is an alignment of core values.

Consider that most people have positive views about Branson and Virgin Airlines because of the core values of Branson and Virgin, namely fairness to customers, also reflect the desires of their customer base. Thus, there is complete alignment between Branson, his companies, and his customers.

The next crucial question is: How is one supposed to think about brand personality and archetypes? Clearly, archetypes are by no means rational. They speak to something different in us, something largely hidden from our view, something intuitive.

If you have been working in your business for a long time, you could be feeling like the late actor Cary Grant who once stated, "I pretended to be somebody I wanted to be until finally I became that person. Or he became me." [C11:7]

The simplest way to begin identifying your archetype is to look to your past. You need to look at where you have been successful. Reflect on your attitude, enthusiasm, and level of passion. Identify how you exceeded your customer's needs. And more importantly, look at how you were communicating about your business—what message were you sending out?

Alignment is the Key

The point we're making is that Branson is in total alignment with his archetype, both in personal and business matters. As a result he is right at home in all that he does. This, in turn, inspires us to trust him and go with his brand.

This too is possible for you and your business. But first you have to figure out your own archetype!

Once this alignment is in place you will be amazed at what's possible. Archetypes are not something that you do, rather you *are* the archetype. When you live and work in this alignment, it will enable your business to emerge wearing its integrity on its sleeve. When you have integrity and shoot straight, people know this intuitively.

This is the true meaning of congruence: To be at peace with your business so it reflects your essence like a mirror.

Once you have found the archetype that most aligns with your true identity, and the needs of your customers, the next step is to focus on everything you say and do toward expressing that archetype through your business efforts.

As we will discuss in the next chapter, success involves avoiding a shotgun approach to business and, instead, being highly focused on your best talents, experience, products, and services.

Without a laser-precise focus, you risk diluting your brand to the point that no one will understand your company or what you stand for.

In the next chapter, we focus on the issue of *focus!*

CHAPTER TWELVE

THE
FOCUSED ENTREPRENEUR

"**W**hen you are inspired by some great purpose, some extraordinary project, all your thoughts break their bonds. Your mind transcends limitations, your consciousness expands in every direction, and you find yourself in a new, great, and wonderful world. Dormant forces, faculties and talents become alive, and you discover yourself to be a greater person by far than you ever dreamed yourself to be."

Patanjali's book, *Mahabhasya (Great Commentary)*

For us, this quote by Patanjali, who was a Hindu during India's Mauryan period, captures the true essence of what is possible through intentional focus and alignment. Because being focused does not mean you only manage one task or one project at a time. On the contrary, focus in this context is about aligning yourself with your higher purpose—the reason you do what you do.

Benefits of Being Focused

With over three hundred branded companies operating in thirty countries, employing fifty thousand people, you'd be right in asking, as many others have, how does Sir Richard Branson stay focused?

The same might have been said of Oprah Winfrey. Over a twenty-five year period, 4,561 days of her life, how has she been able to remain focused?

In both cases, the true benefits of *being* focused and *remaining* focused can only be measured over the long term.

Take for instance the farewell season of The Oprah Winfrey Show. The three-day finale provided the world with an incredible insight into the legacy of Oprah and what her show has been about: Twenty-five years of history-making, life-changing television. [C12:1]

And while we have all been very aware of how amazing and powerful Oprah has become, it is not until you see the impact of one person's commitment and focus that you are able to be totally present and connected with what's truly possible.

What Drives an Entrepreneur?

There is no doubt that Sir Richard Branson and Oprah Winfrey are two very focused individuals. And the reason for providing you with our insights, chapter by chapter, is to awaken the inspiring and extraordinary spirit within you, and encourage you to live a life that you are equally passionate about.

Entrepreneurs are innately driven by success. They are forever engaged in seeking new possibilities and raising the bar. They're always on the verge of something bigger.

It takes a special kind of person to enter the globalized world of business. And as an entrepreneur you understand that operating a small business is no easy triumph. It's time intensive and high-risk. It could be said that running a business is for the brave and courageous—the ones who are willing to soar off a cliff.

Others consider it briefly, and despite the desire for financial freedom, they come to the conclusion that running a business isn't for them. On the other hand, those who have connected with their entrepreneurial spirit see the intensity *and* the risk and know that this is exactly the challenge they are seeking. The world is their oyster and the freedom of choice brings about unlimited possibilities.

Remaining Focused as the World Changes

The entrepreneurial spirit thrives on the fact that the world is forever changing. Change is part and parcel of an entrepreneur's life. Change enables the continual flow of opportunities.

Change challenges the entrepreneur to continually go to their next level. Every year, every month—in fact every day is about experiencing something new and exciting.

However, if an entrepreneur loses their way, becomes unfocused, forgets why they're doing what they're doing, they often become restless, bored and in an extreme case destroy everything that they've ever created. And this is why we challenge you to step up and develop your personal brand and become the leading authority in your niche.

In building your personal brand based on your core values, integrity, and true identity (symbolized by an archetype discussed in the previous chapter), you have the opportunity to live just as fulfilling a life as Sir Richard Branson and Oprah Winfrey.

Your ultimate challenge is to ensure that you are focused, aligned, and congruent with who you are and what you're here to accomplish. Start to realize the impact you will have on this world when you are focused. You are no different than the beam of a laser. When there is focus, your brand remains strong, clear, powerful, and incessant.

Therefore, in order to truly become a business rock star you should begin by focusing on your own specific niche rather than on trying to dominate a whole range of different fields at once. In other words, we claim that the best way to get where you want to go is to keep it *simple* and keep it *focused*.

Your Relationship to Money

Most entrepreneurs think that they are already focused. And they are. However, the focus is on earning more money! And when they look back at their time with the business, it's not uncommon to realize they are now working just as hard, if not harder, to get the same kind of results as before.

Therefore, we want you to consider that money isn't the place to direct your entire focus. Entrepreneurs who focus solely on the dollars will tend to diversify, introduce new products, and create new sources of revenue. However, they also tend to get distracted and unfocused! And it's very easy to fall into this trap. The pressure continues to build until it becomes virtually impossible to think clearly and realize your vision.

For most entrepreneurs, what gets in the way when the focus is on making money alone is that it tends to lead business owners further away from their core values, integrity, and true archetypes—the solid foundation of their business and personal brand—especially if money is not a core value.

Money is important, but equally important is the fact that it is disorientating. It can alter how you perceive the world. It can influence you to do irrational things. The more your eye remains on the money the more your relationship to it changes.

When you become fixated on money, it begins to control you and have an overriding influence on the decisions you make. A positive entrepreneurial ego drives opportunity and successful outcomes. The negative entrepreneurial ego, if left unchecked, is a recipe for disaster.

Focus: The Key Factor in Success

Let's take a closer look at the importance and nature of a healthy focus within a business. Perhaps the best book about this in recent years, a best seller in its own right, comes from Al Ries. It is called *Focus: The Future of Your Company Depends on It.* [C12:2]

Ries discusses the issue of focus, principally in the introduction to the book, using a simple analogy: "The sun is a powerful source of energy. Every hour the sun washes the earth with billions of kilowatts of energy. Yet with a hat and sunscreen you can bathe in the light of the sun for hours at a time with few ill effects."

He continues: "A laser is a weak source of energy. A laser takes a few watts of energy and focuses them in a coherent stream of light. But with a laser you can drill a hole in a diamond or wipe out a cancer.

"When you focus on a company, you create the same effect. You create a powerful, laser-like ability to dominate a market. That's what focusing is all about.

"When a company becomes unfocused, it loses its power. It becomes a sun that dissipates its energy over too many products and too many markets." [C12:3] Yet another powerful lesson from Al Ries is, "Marketing is not selling. Marketing is building a brand in the mind of the prospect." [C12:4]

The meaning of this analogy is pretty straightforward. But marketing is a daunting task, even for multinational companies with millions of dollars available for advertising.

What hope is there for you as a small business owner? How

can you gain that vital space in the mind of your customers and potential ones? In addition to what we've already described in this book, it will take considerable focus!

Own Your Niche

Sergio Zyman, former chief marketing officer at Coca-Cola, once said that, "Everybody has a thousand choices for any product they might want to buy, and there are a million different products competing for their wallets." [C12:5]

With this kind of competition, it's tempting to think that you need to be more diversified. But Ries adds that "A diversified company with many products and services quickly loses sight of its enemy. In truth, it has so many enemies that it cannot keep an eye on any of them. Which is why a diversified company is repeatedly defeated by surprise attacks by its unseen enemies." [C12:6]

The lesson for small business owners is that you do not have the capacity to experiment too much. You cannot engage in ego trips. Even the smallest error in judgment will be paid from your own pocket—it will have a definite, detrimental effect on your bottom line.

The Enemy of Focus

As we examined in our book *The Invisible Entrepreneur*, to stay within such a tight focus can disengage an entrepreneur. Entrepreneurs are focused on pushing into new frontiers, exploring new business territory.

Here are some of the typical counter-productive behaviors of the entrepreneur—all of which can lead to losing that laser-like focus:

- *Have multiple projects and ideas going at the same time*
- *Get frustrated and easily bored*
- *Lack of temperament to manage a company to maturity*

- *Create change and havoc*
- *Operate on instinct*
- *Always keep rolling the dice*
- *Feel an overpowering urge to do it your way*
- *Find yourself not paying enough attention to detail*
- *Find yourself too intent on the dream to recognize the risks*
- *Create problems or a crisis atmosphere*
- *Decide with your heart only, not your heart and head*

These are neither positive nor negative. In fact these behaviors can be advantageous when used powerfully.

Best known for their visionary talents, the entrepreneur excels in the early stages of growth. The project is new, exciting, challenging and rewarding for them. However, just as the project is reaching its peak, the entrepreneur often loses interest because the challenges have disappeared.

At this point, the entrepreneur's desires are redirected to starting a new project, business, or product. If this happens, it might lead them away from the focus they need to succeed in their present enterprise.

What we are proposing is that the entrepreneur gets reconnected with their vision and takes the existing business to the next level rather than starting a new one. And to do this, the entrepreneur must be *focused*.

The Problem with Wearing Too Many Hats

When you first start out in business, it can feel rewarding to wear many hats. As the entrepreneur, you miraculously become the consummate multi-tasker without giving it a second thought. You have everything coming to you and through you—everyone thinks of you as the fountain of all knowledge.

However, at some point every entrepreneur has a reality

Reality check: If you no longer enjoy keeping all the balls in the air then stop operating as the master juggler.

check. We all wake up and realize that a monster that has been created. And we decide that we really only want to wear *one* hat.

The one and only *hat* that we want you to consider wearing is the one of *focus*. And as we pointed out at the beginning of this chapter, we're not talking about stepping back and playing a small game. No. In fact, this is about stepping up to the plate and taking on something much bigger.

Before you find yourself making up all kinds of excuses to justify that random activity was part of your decision to go into business, take a look around. Are you where you thought you'd be? Is your business delivering the results you envisioned?

When we talk about focus and being focused, what we mean is to resist the temptations to develop a range of businesses—unless, as we say, this is part of your BHAG. Focus is about ensuring that your small business has strong foundations before you venture into other areas.

The Role of Your Primary Archetype

After all, Richard Branson did not happen to walk into the business arena with three hundred enterprises! He had a starting point and at that stage he was simply the owner of a small business working according to his core strengths. That's no different perhaps than where you are now.

The purpose for discovering your primary archetype is to allow you to align with your core values and then begin the development of your personal brand and to grow from that foundation. When you know your archetype and have a deep understanding of your core values, you will be well on your way to becoming a focused entrepreneur.

By becoming focused you won't be tempted to chase every wild dream under the sun, not knowing who you are and grasping at anything that might promise increased wealth. You want everything you do to be aligned with *you*.

While it is possible for someone to have characteristics of a few of the archetypes, we all strongly identify with one in particular—our favorite hat as it were. It is this archetype, this hat, which should become your main focus.

Your BHAG Drives Your Focus

Nothing can be achieved without some degree of determined focus. The best way to tackle the business world is to engage it with a laser-like focus that enables you to move swiftly and easily toward your goals.

And you might as well aim high. By setting yourself one hell of a lofty goal—your strong and compelling BHAG—you'll have the impetus for being focused.

Entrepreneurs who do not have strong goals end up floundering about, trying this and that, and never succeeding at anything. A BHAG will keep you aligned with what really matters. There is absolutely no reason why a determined and focused individual should not reach for what seems impossible. And with a strong desire to achieve, most entrepreneurs rise to the challenge.

In our book *The Invisible Partnership: A Blueprint For Successfully Combining Marriage & Business,* we discuss our story of how we came back from the brink of divorce to building an extraordinary and joyful marriage *and* a highly successful business. Equally, in our book *The Invisible Entrepreneur: How to Grow Your Business by Taking 3 Months Off!* we share the trials and tribulations of what it takes to free yourself from your business.

The common thread in both our books is the importance of having a bigger challenge. As we described, William absolutely required a bigger challenge because he was bored and consequently creating havoc in the business, which in turn started to impact our marriage.

But rather than William going off and pursuing an entirely new business venture outside of his focus, the key was to get him focused on building on the existing business and taking it to the next level. The aim is to never stifle the entrepreneurial spirit. It's about deliberately stretching the boundaries, not wider, but higher.

Engage with Your Customers

Richard Branson and Oprah Winfrey both know the importance of their customers and the power of communication. They also know what it is to be committed to service. And in the final episode of Oprah Winfrey's farewell season, she said, "I am aligned to the vision of service." [C12:7]

In essence, this is what Richard Branson has transferred into the way he does business. He has been able to reach his market at a core level. In *engaging* with your customers, you are doing just this.

He didn't stop here. In fact, he didn't *start* here. His ability to authentically connect with his market powerfully was built on the foundation of his archetype. Had he done it any other way, it would have resulted in a very flaky, shallow experience for his customers, and it would have been unsustainable.

You too can create this powerful experience for your clients. When your intention is aligned with the vision of *serving* your clients, this will not only fuel your focus, but it will also come back to you in full force.

We all prefer to do business with people we can relate to—people whose core values align with our own. Regardless of the service or product we are seeking, we want to deal with an organization who cares. Great advertising is not derived from a dishonest approach towards a product. Rather it zeroes in on some unique aspect and establishes an affinity between the product and the customer. If your personal brand is built on your true essence and your core values, then this authenticity will permeate the relationships you build with your customers.

Creating your personal brand is about sharing the essence of who you are—what drives you, what inspires you, and why you're in business. It shows people what you're up for—the difference *you're* committed to making in *their* life.

The Power of Communication

While you are the soul of your business, your customers are the heart—the lifeblood that keeps you doing the extraordinary things you do within your circle of influence. You create this when you are aligned, authentic, and in communication with them.

And what *you* say matters. In the era of e-mail, Facebook, and Twitter, everyone wants to get connected. When Sir Richard Branson and Oprah respond to a Tweet, an e-mail, or a post on Facebook, how does this make *you* feel? Touched, moved, inspired? You feel as though you matter. You feel valued. So, imagine leaving *your* customers with this feeling.

The world is moving ferociously fast, and it's becoming increasingly challenging to maintain our focus on one thing at any time—especially for entrepreneurs who are constantly moving from one adventure to the next. However, if you are to truly align, connect and *serve* your customers, you need to channel your energy and your focus. Where there is alignment, there is magic and you will be *the* unstoppable rock star in your business domain.

The next phase in this journey is focused on the *external work* that is required to launch your personal brand into the market. Starting with the next chapter, we will help you to understand the framework for doing this in a way that is suitable and feasible for small business owners.

CHAPTER THIRTEEN

MARKETING BY EDUCATING

Traditionally, marketing has been a process of getting your products and services known in the marketplace. However, today's consumers are not only looking for companies that offer high quality products, but also companies they can truly trust.

Large companies often have a difficult time building personal rapport and this is why small businesses are well positioned for building closer connections with their clients. This presents a tremendous advantage for small business owners, and it's why we want you to consider using a personal brand as your marketing strategy. Once again, this is why we look to Richard Branson as our role model.

However, before we go any further, let's define the term

"educate" in the context of developing your personal brand.

In its narrow sense, the word educate means to teach with the aim of making a formative impression on the mind, character, or physical ability of an individual. Education is the process by which society deliberately transmits its accumulated knowledge, skills, and values from one generation to another.

The key to marketing with a personal brand is to become a great teacher. Your goal is to make a great impression by serving and educating your customers. And this is entirely feasible for all small business entrepreneurs, not just for a famous business leader like Branson.

Being the Authority in Your Field

Whatever your field, you want people to come to you first. You want to be known as an authority. But how do you become a great teacher?

Obviously, every great teacher needs to be knowledgeable and an experienced authority in a specific professional arena. The problem is that many (if not most) small business owners don't feel like they have much to offer. They don't see themselves as being experts in their field. This, however, is not true, and we will show you why.

Think about it. In this day and age, you know more about your industry or profession than someone like you would have known twenty years ago. If you've been running your business for more than five years, you certainly know more than the average person or your better-informed customers.

And if you've been in business for more than ten years, you absolutely know enough to be an authority in your field. The key here is to value what you know and share this with your customers and potential customers.

Don't let modesty hobble your progress! Most entrepreneurs

are way too modest about their achievements, experience, and knowledge. Be proud of what you know, and have generosity by sharing it. People are intuitive enough to recognize someone who is genuinely well-versed in their subject versus someone who is boastful and ego-driven.

As business coaches, we often encounter clients who undervalue their knowledge and don't see themselves as experts in their fields. And you may well argue that there are people out there who know a whole lot more about your field than you do. This may be true, but it doesn't mean you are not able to be a leading authority in your field.

Challenge your notions of modesty and self-effacement, and dig deep. You're sure to find that you are not only an authority in your field, you could possibly be *the* leading one.

Become a Life-Long Learner

However, this doesn't mean that you can stop learning or that you've reached the pinnacle of your professional and personal development. In fact, you can and should constantly grow as an expert by updating your knowledge and keeping ahead of your competitors.

The more you position yourself as a life-long learner, the more you will be able to serve and educate your customers. By constantly learning, you will be able to offer them the genuine and superior expertise that they value the most.

So take stock of all your experience and knowledge; identify what you know. As we said, you will have accumulated a vast storehouse of valuable information and insights that can then be packaged and offered to your customers as a means of educating them. This will result in increased trust and rapport between you and your customers.

And don't be discouraged about the mistakes of your past. People want to know the juicy stories about what didn't work.

They want to learn from you and they need to be able to relate to you. If your success story is only about the good that has happened to you, people will begin to question their own ability and start to believe that it's probably not possible for them.

Learning from your mistakes is crucial in business, and the lessons of the past can serve to increase your reputation as an expert. Just think of how many great scientists have learned from failed experiments only to later apply all those "failures" toward one incredible success.

In fact, if you are not making mistakes, you are probably playing it too safe. Making mistakes is part of the learning process, and the process of becoming an expert in your field.

Teach What You Know and What Customers Need

The next step in becoming a great teacher and educator is to have a fluent understanding of your customers' needs and circumstances, and to meet those needs with your knowledge and expertise. In short, good education is always a blend of knowing the needs of the students (in this case your customers) and a teacher who has the expertise, knowledge, and experience to provide what the students lack.

It's also crucial for you to ensure there is congruency between your customers' needs, your archetype, and your core values. For instance, from our observations, Branson always seeks to tap into the heart, mind, and pulse of his market. Again, this is his Hero archetype coming into play.

For example, when Virgin Blue, now Virgin Australia, first came to Australia they were like knights in shining armor rescuing us from paying disgustingly high airfares. By understanding the customers' needs, Branson was able to apply his own knowledge and expertise and provide a solution for the Australian market.

Once again, your starting point is to recognize the wealth

of experience and knowledge you already have and embrace yourself as being an authority in your business niche. And then identify your customers' needs as they pertain to your expertise and begin to educate them.

Everyone Has a Story to Tell

Take this book as an example. The subject matter is oriented toward what William was trained in and practiced for over twenty-five years while working with some of the largest ad agencies in Australia.

In fact all of our books are based on our personal experience, professional expertise, and knowledge. For instance, our book *The Invisible Entrepreneur: How To Grow Your Business By Taking 3 Months Off!* is about how you can structure your business to run without depending on your constant involvement. This enables you to take three months off without having to run the business by remote control, by phone, or e-mail.

Before writing *The Invisible Entrepreneur*, we went through a difficult time of being overwhelmed with the demands of our business, to the point that it almost ruined our marriage. We knew we needed some extended time off and therefore we put a plan in place to restructure our business so we would be free to take the time we needed. This became the basis for us to become authorities in that niche.

At the same time, we could see that our problem was common among our clients. Almost everyone felt their businesses were running them instead of the other way around. The more we studied our customers, the more we saw that we could fill a need in their lives by educating them through our book.

However, if we hadn't studied the needs of our customers, we would never have seen the need for the book. And if we hadn't gone through the experience of restructuring our own company, so it would run without us for a few months, our book would have been a sham. We had to have both the knowledge of our customers and the practical expertise to truly serve them.

As it turned out *The Invisible Entrepreneur* has separated us from the other small business coaching companies. We have gained increased rapport and trust from our clients. They see us as a leading authority. And the benefits to our company have been a natural flow-on effect based on our efforts to educate our customers.

The same principle applies to our second book *The Invisible Partnership*. We saw a huge need among life partners, who also run a small business together, to understand how to maintain a successful personal and business relationship without breaking up.

And once again, our expertise in this area proved to serve our clients in a very beneficial way.

Only a couple working and living together can really understand the dynamics that take place in this situation.

The More You Teach, the More You Become an Authority

Both our books were based on our area of expertise, and this has allowed us to be seen as leading authorities. But this didn't require us to go to Oxford for a Ph.D. It simply required us to step out of our comfort zone and embrace a new adventure—while learning as we progressed.

As we wrote our books—they became a form of teaching—and we found we naturally became seen as authorities. The more we taught, the more our existing and potential clients saw us as leading experts. Indeed, that is what we became. So even if you didn't do all that well at school, don't let that stop you from educating your customer base.

There is also an important by-product from teaching your specialty: To do it effectively, you must know your subject even better. So you'll constantly be learning. You will gain even more expertise in the area as you refine your understanding.

You will soon find yourself searching for more information, either through formal education, reading books and articles, or other forms of personal improvement. The more you learn, the more active your brain becomes. You will feel mentally younger, more optimistic, and more alive. As a result, we have seen the confidence of entrepreneurs skyrocket. They gain renewed vigor.

The More You Give, the More You Get

The more knowledge you gain the more you feel you are walking your talk. This is a powerfully upward and enthusiastic trajectory. You will soon exhibit contagious energy. People will be attracted to you. They will come to you for information, advice, and ideas. You become a self-fulfilling prophecy.

From a business perspective, a remarkable thing will begin to occur. If you play your cards right, you may even begin to get calls from journalists as your authority and reputation grows. Think about it. If you are known as an expert in a particular subject, people are likely to turn to you for help and advice. And that will naturally increase your customer base.

It pays to be the expert in your field and here are five key tips that will help you become just that.

Five Tips to Help You Become a Rock Star in Your Field

- **Your knowledge.** Choose one area where you know you have achieved success. For example, your teachings could be based on how to build a business culture based on your core values. Or you could teach on how to be the Hero (like Branson) and do what the masses think is impossible in order to serve your customers. Connect with your customers and ask them what they think your expertise is—what they rely on you for. There is a magic story there.

- **What are you committed to?** What would you do, even if you didn't get paid to do it? Many large organizations have a vision and mission statement, as well as a plaque with their core values listed. However, they're simply paying lip service to them. So identify what you are truly committed to and create a teaching platform around this.

- **What are you inspired by?** Never think that what inspires you won't inspire others. Everyone is looking for a mentor. Believe in what you do and share your inspiration with others. You'll be amazed at the impact you can have on people.

- **Look to others with a good reputation.** If you are not confident enough to stand up as the authority in your own right, a good first step is to consider linking with others who are aligned with your ethics, values, or expertise. This is the strategy we adopted during our early years as coaches. We invited recognized industry experts to speak to our clients. That helped elevate us to their level. This is what is termed as borrowed credibility.

- **Making a difference.** If you are committed to making a difference to the greatest number of people, we highly recommend supporting a charity or an organization that is aligned to your core values.

And we totally understand if all of this sounds too simple. We also realize that we are not only communicating with you, but also with the people on your bus. So allow us to repeat once more that we believe that you have everything you need to become a business rock star. And it starts with valuing the wealth of knowledge and experience you have as an entrepreneur.

You must give value to what you have, and launch yourself from that position. Your foundation is a combination of your knowledge, your core values and your archetype. You need to channel all of these elements into a laser-like focus and package what you have so that you can offer it to your clients in a positive and inspiring way.

Always remember to connect with the needs of your customers and find a natural link between your expertise and their needs. Commit to being a life-long learner who is always growing and seeking self-improvement. The more you grow, the more you will be seen as a trusted expert; and this will attract all kinds of new business to your doors.

In the next chapter, we will share one of the most powerful and effective ways to educate your customers and establish yourself as a rock star in your field: by becoming a published author! If you're ready, then read on!

CHAPTER FOURTEEN

THE ENTREPRENEUR BECOMES AN AUTHOR

Books are like oxygen. They are vital to our existence as human beings. They are the basis for who we are, how we learn, and what we know about the world we live in. Books represent knowledge and are an invaluable contribution to the world. They inspire, educate, and enable us to pass on information from one generation to another.

Books nurture our souls and provide us with great wisdom. They challenge us to grow, expand our way of thinking, and remind us that there will never be a time when we can stop learning.

We have never met an entrepreneur yet that hasn't read at least one business or personal growth book in their life. In fact, it's always very interesting to take a look at an entrepreneur's bookshelf—it's a window to their world.

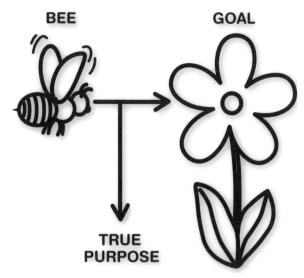

The "Law of Precession" in action.

When entrepreneurs are committed to ongoing professional and personal development, their business thrives. However, when an entrepreneur considers that they know it all, and there's nothing else for them to learn, their business dies.

In the realm of marketing and personal branding, you lift your personal and business credibility by authoring a book. It provides you with the opportunity to catapult you and your business into a whole new dimension. Your book becomes a marketing tool, one that is intrinsically linked to you, your personal brand, your business, and your clients.

Your Opportunity to Inspire Others

Buckminster Fuller,[C14:1] who based his life on a theory called "Law of Precession," stated that for every action we take there is a side effect arising at ninety degrees to the line of our action. He demonstrated this theory using the example of bees.

If you think about pollination, bees do not intend to pollinate, yet they do so and benefit both the bee and the flower. Fuller

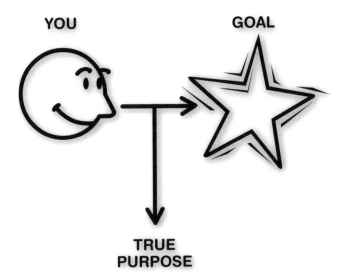

YOU   **GOAL**

**TRUE
PURPOSE**

Your goal is to become a business rock star.
Based on the "Law of Precession" you will make a difference to the greatest number of people
by educating and inspiring them as a published author.

theorized that the bee is getting a reward from nature because it is helping nature to reproduce plant life.

The same is true for you. As a published author you have the opportunity to make a difference to your readers' businesses and lives. We believe the true purpose of a book is to inspire the reader by sharing your story. It should also challenge the status quo, get the reader to think about their life, and above all, propel them into action.

There is no better way for you to share your story than by writing a book. We absolutely know that *anyone* and *everyone* can become an author. However, as we discussed in the previous chapters, you must believe that this is possible.

We also know that your inner dialogue is likely to have kicked in again and is saying that you couldn't possibly become an author. And we know exactly where you're at.

At one point, our not-so-little voices were telling us we couldn't do it either. However, despite our fears, concerns, and trepidation in becoming authors, here you are reading one of our books.

When a friend asked us why we were thinking of writing a book, our answer was simple: If our book made a difference in one person's life, then it was worth all the effort in getting it written and published. So he said, "What are you waiting for? You better get the book done so you can make a difference to that one person." And so we jumped off the cliff and the rest is history.

So thank your inner dialogue for sharing its opinions with you and let's look at the benefits of publishing a book and *why* you would consider becoming an author.

Benefits of Publishing a Book

Publishing a book is first and foremost a marketing initiative. It is no different in principle than having a website, a business card, or a corporate brochure. From a business perspective, there are certainly some very attractive commercial benefits.

But the most important benefit is that, as an entrepreneur, you get to make a difference by sharing your gifts and talents with a larger audience. And, as with your business, you will have a sense of personal pride and achievement in bringing a book to market.

Our books, *The Invisible Entrepreneur* and *The Invisible Partnership* continue to produce great results and, based on the feedback we have received, they have had a positive impact in the lives of our readers. That's just what we wanted. It was our driving force in taking the leap and getting our first book published.

From our perspective, we know the following opportunities are available to you and your business:

- *Strong first impression—people immediately think, "They must know their stuff if they wrote this informative book!"*

- *Adds credibility and will get doors open for you to do business*
- *Raises your profile as a subject matter expert*
- *Increases your ability to gain PR through reviews in both industry press and general media*
- *Increases your ability to gain speaking engagements and appearances on seminar panels*
- *Your book becomes your business card and part of your new client pitch*
- *Serves as an appreciated gift to your existing clients*
- *Enables you to attract the right clients to you*

You may well say that you already enjoy some or all of these benefits. If this is the case, then imagine what is likely to occur if you add a book into the mix.

Another benefit of having a book is that it becomes a silent sales person for your business. It's doing your cold calling, it's drumming up new business opportunities—it's networking for you twenty-four hours a day, seven days a week. It's telling the world how fabulous you are and why they should be doing business with you. And the book never complains or gets bored.

Why Would You Write a Book?

The answer to this question is a very personal one. And it's a decision only you can make. From our perspective, the most honest question you need to ask yourself is: Why would you *not* write a book—especially if you can see merit in developing your own personal brand.

When we were writing our first book, and our little voices kicked in, we kept coming back to this question. Thankfully, at no point did we identify any justifiable reasons for not writing it.

However, let's again look to Sir Richard Branson. He has mastered the genius behind publishing books and understands that marketing goes further than products and services. He's also realized that successful marketing strategies must focus solely on the customer.

Perhaps Richard Branson's reason for writing his first book was to leave a legacy for his children. However, all subsequent books could be seen as his way of contributing to the business community—providing his knowledge and insights about how to grow as an entrepreneur. If you've ever read any of Branson's books, you'll know how invaluable his insights and business tips are for your business and your life.

There is no doubt that writing a book is considered a big, hairy, audacious goal for most people. But for an entrepreneur it's often the next big thing to conquer. But let's be very clear. Do not consider publishing a book purely because you want to make money from book sales. If, of course, you do produce a runaway best seller, then that would be the like the icing on the cake!

From our perspective, the reason for writing a book is that you can make a difference to your customers—existing and prospective. With a book in hand, you can educate and inform your customers—it's a tool to showcase your expertise. A book will become your best ever business card and one that will not be thrown away, especially if you've signed it.

But here's where the true marketing benefit kicks in: Not only will readers remember your book, they're going to remember *you*. It only takes one simple insight to impact them powerfully. This leads them to seek you out and inquire about the products and services you offer. This is where you begin to make money. A great book will cause all this to happen seamlessly.

Like any goal you set, you need to identify your "why," because when you commit to the goal and you know *why* the goal is important to you, then you can take action. When you're clear about this, everything begins to fall into place. You attract the right information at the right time. And you connect with the right people at the right time.

What Should I Write About?

First and foremost your book will be a marketing document. You are not writing fiction, a kid's story, or the adventures of an action hero. You're not trying to show people how clever you are. This is not about going on any ego trip.

The purpose of your book is for you to be seen as the leading authority in your field. You are sharing your knowledge with the world. Therefore, you must write about what you know and what you do because this is about generating more business. The book is your lead generation tool, a profile builder, and a customer classification tool.

As an example, let's use a client of ours who happens to be an accountant. The topic of his book could be *How to Double or Triple Your Profits* or perhaps *How to Turn Your Business into a Money Making Machine*. The focus of his book would be about educating business owners about something that is very important to them—knowing how to be profitable.

If the business owner understands how to do this as a result of reading his book, they're more likely to approach him as a potential customer; they will see him as an expert in his field.

By educating the reader, you will help him or her trust you because you have given them a great deal of information for the price of the book. The precise effect of this is that the accountant gets more inquiries and no doubt a number of these will become new customers.

The benefit to the accountant is that he didn't have to chase for business. Also, his new prospects come with a sense of knowing how he thinks—making it easier to convert them into clients.

Giving is an Act of Generosity

For our previous books, we chose to share our personal experiences—warts and all. *The Invisible Partnership* is about our journey as a married couple and running a business together. We revealed how we contemplated divorce and what it took to create a new platform whereby we could thrive as life partners in business together.

The Invisible Entrepreneur is about our journey of setting up our business so we could take three months off. While the holiday was a bonus for us, this goal enabled us to mature as business owners and reclaim our passion. We knew first-hand that our experience was no different than what other business owners faced. So we decided to share our story in a way that would benefit others.

The topic or context for your book will be as unique as you. No matter what profession or industry you are in, you will have a story to share.

Someone is waiting for you to write your book so they can learn from you. Your story is the gift that could make a profound difference to another human being's life. Generosity is not about how much money or time you give. Giving of yourself is an act of great generosity. And it takes courage because it's risky. The risk, of course, is that you and your message could be rejected. But the rewards far outweigh the risks involved.

To gain clarity on what your book could be about, go back to your personal SWOT analysis, take a look at your strengths, and identify what others rely on you for.

Writing a Book

Writing a book is a lot like eating an elephant; it can only happen one bite at a time. And remember, your book is a marketing document. You are not attempting to write a bestseller or a book that will only be sold at bookstores (unless you're a brilliant writer with an amazing story to tell). You are also not writing *War and Peace*!

Do not turn this project into something that is bigger than Ben Hur because you think that you're probably only ever going to write one book. Once you unleash your inner Branson, you'll realize just how much knowledge you really do have.

In the context of how you write a book, there are two distinct stages. The first is obviously getting your knowledge captured on paper. The second stage is all about what happens with your knowledge, expertise, and wisdom—how it gets packaged and ready for market.

Getting Your Knowledge On Paper

So first, let's look at how you can go about capturing your knowledge. The best method that we have found is for you to talk the book onto your computer, smart phone, or mini-recorder/ dictaphone. Get what you want to say recorded on audio and have someone transcribe it and give you the first draft.

Doing this will speed up the process of writing your book. So don't write your book, speak it. And don't worry about how it comes out. Your first draft won't be perfect (it may even be a bit awful!). Relax. Treat it like a download of content. Even if it's all a bit rough, it's easy to clean up once transcribed.

For those entrepreneurs who are time poor, this is a most effective method. If you consider how much time you spend in traffic driving to and from work, you could literally have the book dictated and transcribed in next to no time.

Another benefit of using this method is that the spoken language is relaxed. Imagine that you're speaking to a colleague or a client. It will also tend to be less stuffy or formal. And, the more relaxed you are, the faster you'll get your ideas down.

The key is to just allow the information to flow, and to not be concerned about the right order.

Now, another way of capturing your thoughts, insights, and knowledge is to do the typing yourself. However, we would only recommend this method if you have a reasonable typing speed. If you're only a two-finger typist, (unless you're very fast) then you're likely to get frustrated and possibly overwhelmed. And if you've got any perfectionism in your blood, you'll want to correct as you go, which will also slow down the process.

If you choose to type your own first draft, the key of course is to just allow your fingers to go with the flow—do not be concerned with typos or structure. Just type as fast as that mind of yours will flow.

Engage the Professionals

Getting your wisdom packaged requires the skills of a team of professionals. Unless you're a very good writer with extensive experience, don't try to craft it all by yourself. We highly recommend that you hire a good editor. Another possibility is to audio tape your thoughts and have someone ghost write your book.

One of the biggest mistakes with our first book was to ask our friends to provide us with feedback. The difference between your friends, family, and colleagues is that your friends are unlikely to give you honest feedback whereas a professional editor will ruthlessly critique your copy and help your book reach a professional level.

Also make sure you hire an editor who is not emotionally involved in the content or feels they need to be nice to you. You must get their honest feedback—that's invaluable. They also need to read from the reader's perspective.

The next team of professionals will be assigned to produce the artwork and graphics for your cover and your typesetting of your manuscript. You must ensure these people have had extensive experience with books.

If they've only done corporate brochures or advertising, you won't get the best outcome. An experienced designer appreciates the subtleties that will make your book look great. We highly recommend that you don't skimp on the look and feel of your book because readers *do* judge a book by its cover. And you must feel proud of your book. If you don't, you won't hand it out.

The style and size of your book will dictate how many chapters you'll need to complete and the time line required for getting your book produced. For instance, a business book could have fifteen chapters, with each chapter containing approximately three thousand words. This would then become a two-hundred page book. In the realm of self-publishing, you get to call the shots. The key question you always need to ask is: What will be most interesting for your market?

What Will Get in Your Way

The short answer is you. And, while there are more reasons why than why not, there are typically two questions that we get asked. First, "How much will it cost?" Second, "How long will it take?" Both these questions are valid.

Money and time are certainly barriers for most entrepreneurs. But if you're smart about this, you will have potential customers paying you to read your marketing document!

The first book is the hardest because there are a lot of unknowns. Producing a book requires patience, tolerance, and commitment to the end result. We also acknowledge that as an entrepreneur your biggest concern might be whether becoming an author would ever produce any real benefits for you and your business. Hopefully we've given you a big enough list of positives for you to consider pursuing this goal.

Another area of concern will be how you'll get this achieved. The thing that most entrepreneurs don't have a lot of is time. However, when an entrepreneur makes a decision to commit to a goal, it's like time stands still. And most entrepreneurs are also great at delegating and enrolling people to help them with their latest cause.

Like any major goal, project, or initiative you need to be disciplined and accountable. One of the best ways to get yourself going is to tell your team or unreasonable friends that you are writing a book and that they can expect a signed copy by a particular date. Once you do this you will find it is particularly difficult not to deliver because you risk losing face in front of everyone.

Your New Business Card

Your key objective is to commit to allocating the time required to get your book published. Because the sooner you get started, the sooner you'll be able to start handing it out.

Your book will become your business card. How impressed will your prospective clients be to receive a copy of your book? How inspired will your current clients be to receive a copy of your newly published book?

There are many hidden benefits to being a published author.

Your book is not only your business card. It is your lead generator, your PR, your keynote presentations, your relationship builder, your credibility, your door opener, your training manual, your elevator pitch, your legacy, and your contribution to making a profound difference in the lives of others.

And most people are aware that it takes guts to write and publish a book, and that it is not for the faint-hearted. Putting your thoughts and ideas in print takes courage.

A book is a way to educate your customers, announce that you are a "rock star" in your field and promote your personal brand. You'll tell the world you are in the business with the top players and at the same time help increase your company's visibility.

You can even use your book as a way of saying thank you to your customers. We have found that people appreciate your book far more than a simple thank-you card. They know these cards costs next to nothing and so your book has far greater impact.

Your book is more than your business card. It's your ticket to becoming a celebrity in your market. Just consider how impressive that is and what it can do for you. So make a decision and start planning your writing schedule today.

In the next chapter, we'll take a closer look at other ways to promote your personal brand and your company.

CHAPTER FIFTEEN

BLOW YOUR
OWN TRUMPET

If you don't blow your own trumpet, no one will. If you're an entrepreneur, then you're in sales and marketing. Your role is to promote, promote and promote—to be seen and get known. No matter how uncomfortable it may be, there is no doubt that you *are* the best spokesperson for your business.

Customers connect with people who are passionate about their business. If you're excited about your business and you communicate why you do what you do, people will want to do business with you. And, above all else, when people know that you are committed to making a difference in their lives, they're even more committed to ensuring that you remain in business.

The curious thing about some entrepreneurs is that they want to be known. However, they do everything possible to ensure they remain unknown. We've read many times over that Richard Branson is an introvert. So if an introvert can create a powerful brand, then there is absolutely nothing that can stand in your way.

Richard Branson has proven that using an unconventional approach to marketing is highly effective. For Branson, PR is not some afterthought grudgingly funded from leftovers scraped from the marketing budget. Public relations is Branson's major communication tool. And there is no doubt that this is a large part of his activities. This is his role and this is what makes the difference.

Make PR a Priority

Today when you think of Branson, you think of Virgin; and when you think of Virgin you think of Branson. Sounds simple when you say it quickly. But it has taken a lot of hard work to make it happen and it didn't happen overnight. However, Branson didn't do it alone—which he is the first to admit.

Branson and Virgin know the importance of having expert PR minds associated with the business. Take for instance Branson's ex-public relations and communications director, Will Whitehorn who recently retired as President of Virgin Galactic.

Whitehorn was a key figure in the development and implementation of Branson's seemingly off-the-cuff stunts and antics—not to mention his serious turns as an industry spokesman when controversies arose or were created.

In the early days, Branson and Whitehorn were always on the lookout for new ways to promote the joint Virgin/Branson brand. Similarly, they kept watchful eyes on possible bad publicity so they could nip it in the bud before the brand could be damaged.

And let's not forget his mentor, Sir Freddie Laker who told

him, "Make a fool of yourself" so Branson would get on the front pages of the newspapers! [C15:1]

Develop a PR Mindset

As a small business owner, you're unlikely to have your own in house PR or branding department. But this doesn't mean you can't adopt some of the strategies that people like Branson have implemented. Branson shows us that his way of using PR is far more cost-effective than some of the traditional media advertising. He has proven that personal branding strategies work.

This is why there is such great value in writing a book. It's an incredibly powerful strategy for personal branding and a great way to educate and serve your customers while establishing yourself as a leader in your field and attracting new clients.

Your book will be a powerful marketing and PR tool for you and your business. It is your calling card, your lead generator. And, as we said, it's your new business card.

It works according to the "loss leader concept," which is often used in retail to get customers into the store. The strategy is to offer one or two products at a price below the seller's cost as a means of attracting customers. Then, while the customer is there, they will inevitably buy other items that bring a profit.

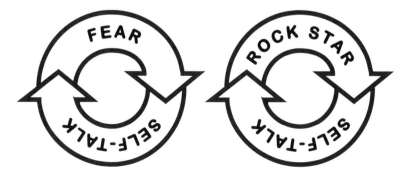

You can continue to listen to the self-talk of fear and struggle.
Or, you can choose to listen to the self-talk of a business rock star.

Give Your Books Away

While your friends and colleagues might think you're crazy for giving books away—don't let that stop you.

This reminds us of the great Apple commercial created in 1997. The message in that commercial is as appropriate today as it was back then. If you haven't seen this commercial titled "Here's to the crazy ones," then you must Google it now. It's also ironic that one of the people featured in that commercial is a younger looking Richard Branson.

Remember that creating your personal brand is about playing a bigger game and bringing clients to your business. And don't discount getting your books sold through distribution channels such as Amazon, and traditional bookshops.

If you're thinking that all of this sounds way out of your comfort zone, then take heed from Branson when he said, "You can't be afraid to take risks." [C15:2] In a small business, if you can develop trust and build a relationship with customers, you can sell a higher dollar value product or service that will generate significant profit.

Your job is to think of all the ways you can get your book into the hands of the right people. As the book opens doors for you, you can build a powerful relationship with your new and existing clients in an even more profitable way.

Focus On Your Target Audience

Choosing your market segment is key. If you're an accountant who specialises in serving entrepreneurs, then you would get your book into the hands of small business owners. If you're a recruitment agency, you would target HR managers or people who are responsible for hiring staff in major companies.

If you're a realtor, your target audience for the book would be people who list properties. And if you're a manufacturer of louvers, you would target architects or interior designers.

The key is to get the attention of the *right* people.

Too often we've seen entrepreneurs make the mistake of thinking they need to spend a lot of money on a large advertising campaign. They usually believe they need to cast a wide net to reach a broad audience in order to increase sales.

From our perspective, we don't believe this is the right approach. Your goal is to become known as the leading authority within your field. Your book, therefore, needs to be distributed among those who could be considered key players in your market segment.

In his best seller *Focus: The Future of Your Company Depends on It*, Al Ries raises the question: "What kind of a niche do you want to own?" [C15:3]

Using an accountant as an example, a more effective way would be to identify a small, manageable number of new clients. He or she might target a group of ten potential clients who would spend on average twelve thousand to eighteen thousand dollars a year.

The goal would be to attract ten triple-A clients, meaning those who would value the accountant's services and be willing to pay fair compensation for those services. And even if the accountant gets just three contracts, the promotional effort would break even in the short term.

However, if you consider the lifetime value of each client, that is the money they will spend during the long term, the return on the accountant's promotional effort would be extremely positive.

In short, casting a wide net may not be the best option for you. It's usually far better to zero in on a smaller target audience and use personal branding to build trust with your clients.

The right doors will open easier than you think.

Promotional Strategies

Once you've identified your target market, it's important to work patiently. You can't expect to achieve everything instantly. It's important to start out on a low incline path, to take one step at a time.

Mount Everest climbers don't start out on the steepest part of the mountain. They start out slow. By setting small, easily achievable initial targets, your risk will be kept to a minimum.

Once you have some success under your belt, you become increasingly able to take bigger risks. However, the process involved in bigger or smaller risks is similar. The key difference is your risk tolerance.

As a small business entrepreneur there are many cost-effective ways to promote your business and your expertise. The key, however, is not to try too many things at once. And, as always, engage the right people with the right experience to support you. We also highly recommend that you focus on the areas where you are likely to excel.

The key areas that have produced extraordinary opportunities for us are: online promotions, networking, speaking engagements, and PR. So, let's take a brief look at each of these areas.

Online Promotions

Broadcasting your business and your expertise has never been easier. Technology has become so user-friendly there really is no excuse for you not to be seen or known.

A great place to start is with your website. More and more websites are utilizing the power of videos and there is enormous scope for you to communicate your expertise.

For instance, one video could be a message from you as the company CEO. Another video could be a series of testimonials from customers talking about your products and services. You could even take a chapter from your book and give the viewer a snapshot of what they'll get from reading your book.

We have deliberately set up our websites so they are full of videos in which people talk about our books and how our books helped them. We can now approach other leaders in our field to provide content for the website far more easily than before. And remember, we got to this stage with the aid of a couple of books.

In addition to videos, we'd also encourage you to have downloads such as articles and tips. And remember: The more you give away, the more they'll keep coming back for more.

However, don't attempt to do this on your own, even if you have the expertise to do so. Your value to your business is worth more than uploading content.

Networking

While a lot of networking occurs online in the social media space, networking events still provide you with an invaluable opportunity to connect with your target audience. Just imagine when someone asks you what you do as a profession. Your answer can be something like, "I am an accountant and a published author. I specialize in helping businesses to become money making machines."

However, we fully appreciate that not everyone is a natural at networking, or enjoys the experience of mixing in large groups. If this is the case, then one strategy that you can adopt is to get involved in the network. Put yourself forward as an invaluable resource. This not only allows you to meet the members at a completely different level, but also supports you to get comfortable in such a setting.

Most networking groups are more than grateful to have business owners who want to get involved. And you could also look at donating a few copies of your book as giveaways.

However, it's important to recognize that networking is about building long-term relationships. If you attend one meeting only, you're unlikely to get any long-term results. If you commit to attending every event possible, then the results will speak for themselves.

Speaking Engagements

As a published author you are more likely to be invited to be a guest speaker by different groups such as the Chamber of Commerce, BNI, small business associations, and networking events. You'll be surprised at just how many speaking opportunities, locally and nationally, will open up for you.

The key is to access a database of all the networking events and to send them your details. Getting this database together should not cost you any money as the information is freely available through a Google search.

However, you don't always have to rely on other events or organizations. You can stage your own events and seminars, as well as set up Webinars and have podcasts available for download. Your seminars can be about anything related to your field, including for the purpose of demonstrating a new product or an innovation. These events will help you educate your prospect and client base.

They also do not need to be conducted by you. You can be the host and let your team run the event. You can invite your customers or someone from within your industry to be the guest speaker. There are so many avenues open to you. If you are pressed for ideas, ask the question "What would Richard Branson do if he was in this position?"

Now imagine being asked to speak at the local Chamber of Commerce. This is, in fact, an opportunity to make a sales pitch.

But rather than just talking one-on-one with a single prospect, you will be able to talk to twenty or more. And this is exactly what happens when Branson is being interviewed on TV or getting on the front page of a newspaper. He does it again and again. So can you.

Every time we see Branson, we get a mental image of the Virgin brand—at a much lower cost than the millions spent by clients of ad agencies trying to achieve the same result. All we invite you to consider is being Branson on a smaller scale.

Use PR to Your Advantage

As the owner of a small business you may not be used to being interviewed or written about. With a book in hand, getting PR is a lot easier than you think. This is all publicity for your product and service, but you might be rather shy about all the attention.

What a business owner can take to heart is that Branson is innately an introvert. Who he is today is very much a result of learned behavior. Look into his eyes; you can see he would rather be doing his own thing within the comfort of his inner circle.

No matter what it is, or even how extroverted you might be, any new thing requires practice. And we learn from our mistakes. Nevertheless, as an author it will be easier for you to get the attention of the media. Your local newspaper and radio station are always looking for good content. So take advantage of this free PR. But remember: in this situation you are the content. So you need to capitalize on the opportunities, and if you are not used to operating in this arena, as it is a specialized skill, we recommend you consider finding a suitable PR firm or consultant who can help you work well with media attention.

"If you challenge yourself you will grow. Your life will change. Your outlook will be positive. It's not always easy to reach your goals but that's no reason to stop. Never say die. Say to yourself, 'I can do it. I'll keep on trying until I win.'" Richard Branson [C15:4]

Remember Your "Why"

As you begin to create your personal brand based on the strategies we have described in this book, it is easy to forget your overall purpose and mission. We encourage you to stay focused on what's important. Your *why* will keep you motivated as you step out of your comfort zone.

Though Branson is perceived as being radical, he says he had to force himself to make speeches, embrace the photo opportunities and take part in the public relations extravaganzas.

He says, "I had to train myself into becoming more of an extrovert." In regard to getting PR, appearing on TV, or showing up on newspaper front pages, Branson says, "It would be bloody stupid to say no." [C15:5]

There's a great story of a person who suffered badly with vertigo. This man was standing at the edge of a ten-story building, where a plank extends from the edge. It was a sheer drop.

At the edge of this six-meter extension, someone stuck a $50 bill and invited the man to walk the plank to get it. If he did, he would get the fifty dollars as a reward. Obviously, he refused.

They then increased the reward to fifty thousand dollars. Still the man said "No." But as the reward was increased, the man was less and less hesitant in refusing the reward. Finally, when the reward got to $500,000, he simply couldn't refuse.

If you were to take on this journey of discovering your own inner Branson, it too will feel like deciding to step out onto that plank. You will have fears, doubts and concerns. And, you will choose to turn back or choose to walk the plank. For this reason you need to be confident about your "why." The "why" of your business will help you transcend your fears and reach the other side in no time.

So stay connected to your BHAG, your core values, your true identity, and your purpose. Your success is up to you. As we said, if you don't blow your own trumpet, no one else will. So get out there and promote, promote and promote. Begin to tell the world your story.

CHAPTER SIXTEEN

FROM ORDINARY TO EXTRAORDINARY

Let's imagine that tomorrow you and your team are being granted an extraordinary gift—the opportunity to learn from one of the greatest entrepreneurs of our times.

The question is: If you and your team were told that Sir Richard Branson was coming to meet with you at your business, then what would your priority be today? Would you be rushing around cleaning up your premises, clearing your desks, getting things in order, and fixing up those little housekeeping issues that have been bugging you for years?

Or would you be brainstorming with your team about how to take full advantage of this opportunity of spending time with Branson, and identifying the key questions you would want to ask him? And more importantly, what would you and your team be committed to doing differently as a result of meeting with him?

Ideally, you'd be empowered with the right mindset and attitude toward your business. You'd no doubt love to see your team step up and take ownership of a new and exciting future. Hopefully, you'd be inspired to create a rewarding partnership with your customers. At the very least, you'd be committed to doing whatever you could to take your business to the next level.

What If You Ran Your Business with a Branson Mindset?

Why wait for the *real* Richard Branson to arrive? Why not lead your business with a Branson mindset today and see the results you can produce? The difference between where you are and where you would like your business to be is a choice that only you can make.

It's time to stop thinking that the grass looks greener on the other side. Stop wishing that you could be like someone else and be willing to drop your mask and take charge of any negative self-belief. We've spoken about your inner dialogue and how those voices tell you "I couldn't do that," or, "If I just work harder, then maybe I'll succeed."

When you decide to take control of your negative "I can't do this" thinking and start focusing on designing a life that you love, then you will be unstoppable. When you choose to honor, value, and respect your unique talents, then anything is possible.

However, if you choose to underestimate your skills and potential, you will only continue along the path of mediocrity.

Throughout this book, we've been challenging you to think differently and to start realizing your true potential. If you don't nurture your strengths, who will? And saying the busyness of running your business prevents you from excelling is no longer an excuse.

Take this opportunity to sit down with your team and have a think-tank session today and ask yourselves: If Sir Richard

Branson walked into your business today, what would he say about your present circumstances? How would he go about running your business? How would he tackle your current challenges?

After all, the qualities that you most admire about Richard Branson are also within you. Physically, there is no difference between you and Branson. He also has exactly two hundred and six bones inside his skin bag. However, mentally there is a big difference.

By learning to operate with a Branson mindset, and by living outside your comfort zone, then anything is possible for you and your business. For instance, when we ask our clients to think with a Branson mindset, these are some of the things they say about what they'd do differently in their businesses:

"I would have fun running my business."
"I'd spend more time on marketing."
"I'd set up the business so that I can do the things that I love the most."
"I'd operate like the CEO rather than the Office Junior."
"I'd enjoy taking on the next challenge, and the next challenge."
"I'd create a bigger vision and be inspired about leaving a legacy."

If there is anything to be learned from Sir Richard Branson it is that if you don't try, then nothing will happen. Reaching for the stratosphere is not something that is only available to people such as Branson. It's available to everyone.

Don't Follow the Masses

George Bernard Shaw said, "Reasonable people adapt themselves to the world. Unreasonable people attempt to adapt the world to themselves. All progress, therefore, depends on unreasonable people." [C16:1]

Many entrepreneurs, despite their strong desire for business success, invent too many reasons for why their dreams cannot be accomplished. The most common excuses are: not enough money, not enough time and not having the right people on their team. These are all reasonable, and justifiable excuses. Unfortunately, they only lead to a negative outcome. They don't focus on the unlimited opportunities that are available. And, they keep you operating like everyone else within your industry.

In the true sense of the word, Branson is an unreasonable person. He says, "My interest in life comes from setting myself huge, apparently unachievable challenges and trying to rise above them . . . From the perspective of wanting to live life to the full, I felt that I had to attempt it." C16:2

This statement illustrates that your greatest opportunities require you to see what you're truly capable of. And most entrepreneurs are quick to state that they're playing a "big" game. However, are they really striving for their personal best in business and in life?

Eleni Gabre-Madhin, an inspiring woman and economist, who is the Chief Executive Officer of the Ethiopia Commodity Exchange (ECX) says, "We spend most of our lives cutting down our ambitions because the world has told us to think small. Dreams express what your soul is telling you, so as crazy as your dream might seem—even to you—I don't care: You have to let that out." C16:3

Your success in business will depend entirely upon your level of unreasonableness. Therefore, the biggest challenge for you, and equally the biggest opportunity for you, is to decide how unreasonable you are going to be in your business and in your life. And being unreasonable begins with taking responsibility for all areas of your life.

The World is Your Oyster

When you decide to live your life by doing the things that you love, you will connect with your inner Branson. As the great French poet Victor Hugo, wrote, "Nothing else in the world . . . not all the armies . . . is so powerful as an idea whose time has come." [C16:4]

For most entrepreneurs, a key reason for starting their own business is because of the desire for freedom and the possibility of creating a life they love. It's also about proving that they're capable of achieving greater things in life. Most entrepreneurs are not accustomed to playing safe, but there is no doubt that when they are not creating their next challenge they can become disillusioned with business, and sometimes life.

Once you have an established business, are confident of your skills and expertise, are surrounded by great people, and are making a decent living, then the search for something more meaningful and challenging starts to raise its head. This is why we invite our clients to look at their business and their life in a holistic way.

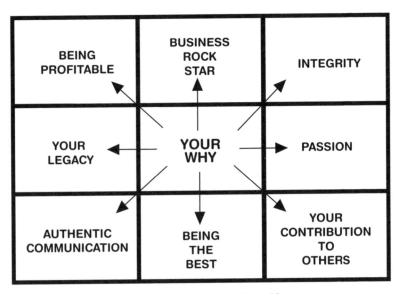

Your "Why" is the foundation for your life.

The previous illustration provides you with an overview of nine key areas in your life. What is important to understand is that every decision must be made from the center of your universe, your "why."

It is for this very reason that we encourage our clients to develop their own personal brand and empower themselves to become the "rock star" in their niche. As we've said, when the entrepreneur is inspired and motivated, so too is the team. The more enjoyment that an entrepreneur is experiencing in business, the more successful their business becomes. And with success comes opportunity.

As a result of reading *The Invisible Branson*, may you be inspired to adopt the principles we have shared with you into your business and your life, and may you truly know that there is nothing that can stop you from becoming the rock star in your business niche.

The best advice that we could ever give you is that there is never any shortage of opportunities available to you when you are open to receiving them. Anything and everything that you desire will flow as a result of doing what you love.

Be inspired by your greatness and be willing to leave behind a huge wake as you sail through life.

And above all else, acknowledge that you are as unique and talented as Sir Richard Branson. As he himself says:

"I am no different than you."
Sir Richard Branson [C16:5]

MOMENT-TO-MOMENT CHOICES

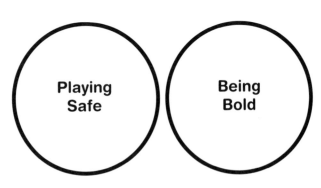

Playing Safe

Being Bold

Think Big

Richard Branson has taken huge calculated risks and equally reaped huge rewards. Twelve months from today will you be in the same place, with the same issues, or will you have catapulted your business, and your life, to a whole new level?

Brainstorm anything and everything that you would like to achieve and then take action today!

....
....
....
....
....
....
....
....
....
....
....
....
....
....

MOMENT-TO-MOMENT CHOICES

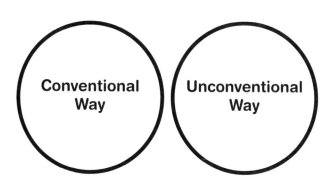

Your Enemy is Convention

As an entrepreneur you get to call the shots. You have the freedom to do it your way. However, it's easy to get stuck and forget that you're in charge of your business and your life.

Branson's philosophy is to defy convention. If you were to live life as an adventure, and got to make money along the way, what would your business and your life look like?

....

....

....

....

....

....

....

....

....

....

....

....

....

....

MOMENT-TO-MOMENT CHOICES

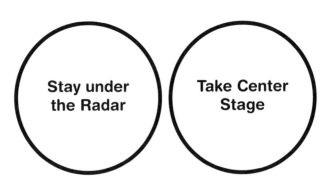

Stay under the Radar

Take Center Stage

Become the Face of Your Business

When you think of Virgin, you think of Sir Richard Branson. How can you become the face of *your* business?

Be proud of your business and what you stand for. Decide to have some fun and unleash your inner Branson. And along the way, be okay about blowing your own trumpet!

....
....
....
....
....
....
....
....
....
....
....
....
....
....

GRATITUDE

The *Invisible Branson* is the result of an extraordinary team of people who have selflessly worked along side us. They are people who are inspired, passionate, and dedicated to empowering entrepreneurs to reach their true potential.

They are unconditionally aligned with the vision of making a difference to the community of small business entrepreneurs. They are our unreasonable mentors, friends, and colleagues, and we are in gratitude for their support, friendship, and generosity. We are grateful that they chose to walk this journey with us.

Firstly, we acknowledge and give thanks to you, Mark and Nick. Heroes in your own right, behind the scenes, you truly made *The Invisible Branson* possible and supported us in bringing our vision to life. You are a living testament of honoring your word. Thank you.

Secondly, we want to thank Lee Iacocca. We are truly blessed and humbled by your generosity. From the bottom of our hearts we thank you for providing the Foreword for *The Invisible Branson*. We are moved by your commitment to making a difference to the lives of others.

Norma Saken, you have been incredible throughout this journey—you are an absolute powerhouse! We thank you for being the angel that you are and we both feel incredibly grateful to have you in our lives.

Phil Atkinson, we thank you for your unwavering and unreasonable commitment around the brilliant cover design of *The Invisible Branson*.

Our incredibly dedicated editors: Andy Otes, Glenn McMahan, and Victoria Leontios. You made bringing this book to life a pleasure. Your wisdom and support has been the difference that made the difference.

Ken Yap, our Financial Controller. We thank you for your leadership and support in managing our business, which has given us the freedom to channel our energy into this book.

All the luminaries: Archbishop Desmond Tutu, Brian Tracy, Al Ries, Dr. Stephen Lundin, Ron Kaufman, and Tony Buzan. We thank you for your selflessness in endorsing *The Invisible Branson*. You've inspired us to be our best and are a living expression of true generosity.

Our Australian support team: Jowel Bondoc, Murray Vanderveer, Jon Hawley, Darren Strauss, Michael Lenton, Julia Kuris, VK, Cecelia Haddad, Kimberly Newman, Gavin Larkin, Andrew Folos and Frank Demaria. Our USA team support: Matthew Hudson and Eric Austin. We thank you.

We want to thank our clients: past and present. We truly value the opportunity to make a difference to you and your businesses. And, we thank you for the contribution you make to us, and our business.

We would also like to thank our teachers and mentors: Dr Barbara De Angelis, Werner Erhard, and Landmark Education. You have made a profound difference to us and who we are today is a result of your teachings and wisdom. Our lives are enriched because of who you are and what you stand for.

Finally to Sir Richard Branson. We thank you for being the inspiring entrepreneurial spirit that you are. May you continue to illuminate the path for others.

Louise & William

REFERENCE NOTES

Chapter One

C1:1 Copyright, Ron Kaufman
Reprinted with permission. Ron Kaufman is the world's leading educator and motivator for uplifting customer service and building service cultures. Ron is the author and founder of UP! Your Service. Learn more at www.UpYourService.com and www.RonKaufman.com.

C1:2 Quote source: http://www.brainyquote.com/quotes/authors/g/gene_simmons.html

C1:3 *Positioning: The Battle For Your Mind,* Authors: Al Ries and Jack Trout McGraw-Hill; 1 edition (December 13, 2000) ISBN-10: 9780071373586

C1:4 Walter Landor (9 July 1913 – 9 June 1995) founder of Landor Associates. Pioneer in the field of branding and consumer research.

C1:5 The Remington brand of razor was originally produced by a division of Remington Rand, starting in 1937. Sperry Corporation sold the division in 1979 to Victor Kiam, who became the company spokesman of the new Remington Products Company. Source: Wikipedia.

C1:6 Jim Collins: An American business consultant, author, and lecturer on the subject of company sustainability and growth. Jim Collins is the author of several books: *How the Mighty Fall: And Why Some Companies Never Give In, Built to Last: Successful Habits of Visionary Companies, and Good to Great.*

C1:7 Richard Branson: *Losing My Virginity: How I've Survived, Had Fun, and Made a Fortune Doing Business My Way,* Crown Business; 1 edition (October 19, 1999), ISBN-10: 9780812932294

Chapter Two

C2:1 *Richard Branson Screw It, Let's Do It: Lessons In Life*—Page 29
ISBN 0-7535-1099-5, Virgin Books (May 16, 2006)

C2:2 *Richard Branson Screw It, Let's Do It: Lessons In Life*—Page 13
ISBN 0-7535-1099-5, Virgin Books (May 16, 2006)

Chapter Three

C3:1 *Star Wars: Episode V—The Empire Strikes Back* (1980)

C3:2 *Built to Last: Successful Habits of Visionary Companies* Authors: James Collins and Jerry Porras, HarperCollins Publishers; 1st edition (January 15, 1997) ISBN-10: 0887307396

C3:3 Quote source: http://www.allvoices.com/contributed-news/5863389-greatness-lives-on-the-edge-of-destruction

C3:4 Guillaume Apollinaire (26 August 1880 – 9 November 1918), a French writer of Italian birth and Polish descent, was hugely influential as a Modernist poet and as a spokesman for the Cubist painters.

C3:5 Albert Schweitzer (14 January 1875 – 4 September 1965) was a German (Alsatian) theologian, organist, philosopher, physician, and medical missionary.

C3:6 Sophocles; c. 497/6 BC – winter 406/5 BC, is one of three ancient Greek tragedians whose plays have survived. His first plays were written later than those of Aeschylus, and earlier than those of Euripides.

C3:7   Michelangelo di Lodovico Buonarroti Simoni (6 March 1475 – 18 February 1564), commonly known as Michelangelo, was an Italian Renaissance painter, sculptor, architect, poet, and engineer.

C3:8   Virgin Galactic is the world's first spaceline. http://www.virgingalactic.com/booking/

C3:9   Quote source: http://www.brainyquote.com/quotes/quotes/r/richardbra371285.html

Chapter Four

C4:1   Albert Einstein: (14 March 1879 – 18 April 1955) was a German-born theoretical physicist who developed the theory of general relativity, effecting a revolution in physics.

C4:2   As seen in article: http://www.csmonitor.com/World/Olympics/2010/0222/For-many-Vancouver-Olympics-athletes-sports-psychology-is-key

C4:3   Sir Frederick Alfred Laker (6 August 1922 – 9 February 2006) was a British airline entrepreneur, best known for founding Laker Airways in 1966. Laker SkyTrain Laker Airways was a wholly private, British independent airline founded by Sir Freddie Laker in 1966.

C4:4   Quote source: http://www.buddhistchannel.tv/index.php?id=18,1271,0,0,1,0)

Chapter Five

C5:1   George Bernard Shaw (26 July 1856 – 2 November 1950) was an Irish playwright and a co-founder of the London School of Economics.

C5:2   *The Tragical History of Hamlet, Prince of Denmark,* or more simply *Hamlet,* is a tragedy by William Shakespeare, believed to have been written between 1599 and 1601.

Chapter Six

C6:1   George Bernard Shaw (26 July 1856 – 2 November 1950) was an Irish playwright and a co-founder of the London School of Economics

C6:2   *Richard Branson: Losing My Virginity: How I've Survived, Had Fun, and Made a Fortune Doing Business My Way,* Crown Business; 1 edition (October 19, 1999), ISBN-10: 9780812932294

C6:3   Quote source: http://www.brainyquote.com/quotes/quotes/m/magicjohns227547.html

C6:4   Quote source: http://www.brainyquote.com/quotes/keywords/doing_10.html

Chapter Seven

C7:1   Quote source:
http://www.thisismoney.co.uk/home/article.html?in_article_id=410885&in_page_id=1

C7:2   Quote source:
http://www.virgin.com/entrepreneur/news/wanted-the-caribbean-richard-branson

C7:3   Quote source:
http://thinkexist.com/quotation/life_is_either_a_daring_adventure_or_nothing-to/13581.html

C7:4   Quote source:
http://www.openforum.com/videos/branson-on-business-criteria-for-a-virgin-brand-inside-the-entrepreneurial-mind-series

C7:5   The term Big Hairy Audacious Goal ("BHAG") was proposed by James Collins and Jerry Porras in their 1996 article entitled *Building Your Company's Vision.*

Chapter Eight

C8:1 Quote source:
http://www.virgin.com/about

C8:2 Quote source:
http://www.virgin.com/about

C8:3 The Art of Demotivation Author: E.L Kersten ISBN: 1892503417, Despair Inc, 2005

C8:4 *Built to Last: Successful Habits of Visionary Companies* Authors: Jim Collins, Jerry I. Porras, HarperCollins Publishers; 1st edition January 15, 1997 ISBN: 100887307396

C8:5 Quote source:
http://www.virginaustralia.com/AboutUs/Careers/Cultureandvalues/

C8:6 Quote source:
http://www.thebodyshop.co.uk/_en/_gb/services/aboutus.aspx

C8:7 Quote source:
http://www.thebodyshop.com/_en/_ww/services/aboutus.aspx

C8:8 Quote source:
http://www.quotationspage.com/quote/31264.html

C8:9 Quote source:
http://www.guardian.co.uk/business/2006/mar/17/retail.money

C8:10 Quote source:
http://www.brainyquote.com/quotes/quotes/a/alberteins121993.html

Chapter Nine

C9:1 Quote source:
http://www.brainyquote.com/quotes/quotes/j/johnfkenn109213.html

C9:2 Quote source:
http://www.mountainman.com.au/gaia_jim.html

C9:3 Quote source:
http://www.goodreads.com/author/quotes/546897.Linda_Ellis

Chapter Ten

C10:1 Definition source:
http://oxforddictionaries.com/definition/morality

C10:2 *Good to Great: Why Some Companies Make the Leap... and Others Don't* Author: Jim Collins, Publisher: HarperBusiness; 1 edition (October 16, 2001), ISBN-13: 978-0066620992

C10:3 *Education Through Recreation* Author: Lawrence Pearsall Jacks. Reprint published by Harper & Row, New York. ISBN: 0834304280

C10:4 Quote source:
http://www.strategicbusinessteam.com/famous-small-business-quotes/richard-bransons-quotes-famous-business-quotes-from-the-builder-of-the-virgin-group-brand/

Chapter Eleven

C11:1 Quote source:
http://en.wikipedia.org/wiki/Archetype

C11:2 Quote source:
http://en.wikipedia.org/wiki/Carl_Jung

C11:3 Quote source: Archetypes via BrandHouse Denmark http://www.brandhouse.com/Web/EN/Archetypes/The+12+archetypes

C11:4 Quote source:
http://joannapenabickley.typepad.com/on/2007/06/on_the_12_arche.html

C11:5 Quote source:
http://www.archetypal-branding.com

C11:6 Quote source:
http://www.nytimes.com/1993/12/22/business/domino-s-ends-fast-pizza-pledge-after-big-award-to-crash-victim.html

C11:7 Quote source:
http://thinkexist.com/quotation/i_pretended_to_be_somebody_i_wanted_to_be_until/201385.html

For additional recommended reading on this subject:
Dr Carol S. Pearson and Jungian archetypes link: http://en.wikipedia.org/wiki/Jungian_archetypes

Chapter Twelve

C12:1 Quote source:
http://www.oprah.com/oprah_show.html

C12:2 *Focus: The Future of Your Company Depends on It* Author: Al Ries, Harper Paperbacks (September 27, 2005) ISBN-10: 0060799900

C12:3 *Focus: The Future of Your Company Depends on It* Author: Al Ries, Harper Paperbacks (September 27, 2005) ISBN-10: 0060799900

C12:4 *Focus: The Future of Your Company Depends on It* Author: Al Ries, Harper Paperbacks (September 27, 2005) ISBN-10: 0060799900

C12:5 *The End of Marketing As We Know It,* Author: Sergio Zyman Publisher: Harper Paperbacks (November 7, 2000) ISBN-10: 9780887309830

C12:6 *Focus: The Future of Your Company Depends on It* Author: Al Ries, Harper Paperbacks (September 27, 2005) ISBN-10: 0060799900

C12:7 Quote source:
http://www.oprah.com/oprah_show.html

Chapter Fourteen

C14:1 Quote source:
http://en.wikipedia.org/wiki/Buckminster_Fuller

Chapter Fifteen

C15:1 Quote source:
http://www.guardian.co.uk/news/blog/2006/feb/10/post75

C15:2 Quote source:
http://www.hrh.ch/whoiswho/bransonr/br_page5.html

C15:3 *Focus: The Future of Your Company Depends on It* Author: Al Ries, Harper Paperbacks (September 27, 2005) ISBN-10: 0060799900

C15:4 *Richard Branson Screw It, Let's Do It: Lessons In Life—Page 39* ISBN 0-7535-1099-5, Virgin Books (May 16, 2006)

C15:5 Quote source:
http://www.hrh.ch/whoiswho/bransonr/br_page4.html

Chapter Sixteen

C16:1 Quote source:
http://thinkexist.com/quotation/reasonable_people_adapt_themselves_to_the_world/206564.html

C16:2 Quote source:
http://www.highstakesliving.com/richard-branson.html

C16:3 Quote source:
http://en.wikipedia.org/wiki/Eleni_Zaude_Gabre-Madhin

C16:4 Quote source:
http://www.unitedearth.com.au/hugo.html

C16:5 Quote source: Perth Event—May 2010

THE INVISIBLE ENTREPRENEUR
HOW TO
GROW YOUR BUSINESS BY
TAKING 3 MONTHS OFF!

"Full of powerful, practical advice that any business owner can immediately use to increase their profits and reduce their work hours. I wish I had this book twenty years ago, it would have made building my business a lot easier."
— ***Siimon Reynolds**, Co founder, Photon Group*

When was the last time you took three months off? If you are the owner of a small business, taking an extended holiday may seem like an audacious and impossible goal. But the problem is not your business. It's you.

That's why *The Invisible Entrepreneur* is an absolute must read for anyone intent on succeeding without letting their business dominate their life.

Have you ever wondered how Sir Richard Branson, founder of the Virgin Group, can head up three hundred or so businesses and still take time to enjoy life? We certainly wondered, because at one point in our life we struggled just to keep one small business running profitably. We were simply slaves to our business.

There is no doubt that Richard Branson is the ultimate

"invisible entrepreneur." He has been able to separate himself from his businesses so that they can run without depending on him and the same is possible for you.

The Invisible Entrepreneur pinpoints one of the biggest mistakes that business owners make. They deliberately build a business that traps them, and then they fight to maintain their limitations. But once you realize this, you will never run your business the same way again.

In this book you will learn:

- *Why the conventional wisdom of simply setting up systems and processes, however good they are, will not free the business owner from constant hands-on involvement.*
- *How you can take three months off, or more, by learning to manage risks.*
- *Why it's essential to have the right people in place and how you can recruit and build a team you can rely on.*
- *And, how taking three months off can actually make your business stronger.*

We will challenge you to take a hard look at the way you keep yourself trapped. We'll encourage you to look to your future—to see that you could actually fail if you don't start making changes.

All of the information in this book is highly focused, extremely practical, and above all, readily applicable. We help you make the important changes that your business needs in order for you to take three months off, or more.

Your business should be a money-making machine, not a prison. *The Invisible Entrepreneur* will help you create the freedom to bring out your inner Branson. Learn to let your business work for you, instead of you working for your business. And yes, you can have fun while making money.

THE INVISIBLE PARTNERSHIP
A Blueprint For Successfully Combining Marriage & Business

"Successfully working with a spouse is both a tricky and complicated process. The Invisible Partnership provides wise, constructive teachings that will help to strengthen your relationship and lead you onto the road to accomplishment."

— Stephen R. Covey
"The 7 Habits of Highly Effective People" and "The Leader in Me"

I s it really possible for life partners to successfully live, love, and work together? The answer is: Yes.

The Invisible Partnership is based on our story, told honestly with no holds barred. And while these experiences are ours, we know they are not ours alone. When *The Invisible Partnership* came out, we were astounded to hear from so many readers that our book resonated with them. They told us that this book changed their business and their lives. We hope that it can change yours.

We look at the conflicts that arise within a life partnership/ business partnership relationship due to being together 24/7 when there's no escaping each other. We explore how you can harness your individual talents and become an unstoppable force.

We also openly discuss how you can operate as powerful leaders without compromising each other or holding each other back.

Here are just a few of the lessons and insights that this book explores:

- *By combining, instead of separating work and home, you can energize both "worlds" in ways you never imagined.*
- *Disagreements at work need never spill over into the home; rather, they can be the building blocks of a new level of communication.*
- *Normal management theories don't work in businesses run by life partners. We look at the reasons for this and by understanding the unique operating principles, you can avoid the pitfalls.*

The Invisible Partnership is an invaluable resource for anyone in business, or who is thinking of going into business with someone else. So whether you are romantically involved, family members, best friends or simply joined through business—this book is for you and your business partner.

We will help you structure your company so you can work together and value each other's strengths. We will help you see that it is possible to work collaboratively and respectfully, without stepping on each other's toes and without driving each other crazy.

The Invisible Partnership is a journey of transformation. Each chapter will lead you on a journey of self-discovery. You will learn that you don't have to sacrifice your relationship for your work. Nor do you have to sacrifice yourself. And, it's possible to follow both your head in business and your heart in love.

THE INVISIBLE BRANSON IS ALSO AVAILABLE IN:

- Audio Book
- E-Book
- Kindle Edition
- Smashwords
- Amazon.com

Please visit our websites and subscribe to the fortnightly newsletter today!

- www.InvisibleBranson.com
- www.QuantumPublications.com.au
- www.InvisibleBlog.com